C000295876

LAND ROVER
Emergency Vehicles

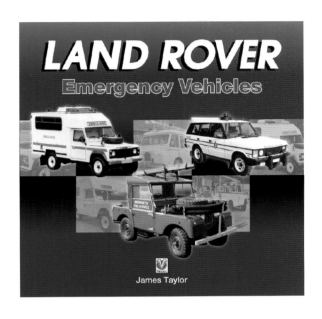

James Taylor

More from Veloce:

SpeedPro Series

4-Cylinder Engine Short Block High-Performance Manual – New Updated & Revised Edition (Hammill)
Aerodynamics of Your Road Car, Modifying the (Edgar and Barnard)
Camshafts – How to Choose & Time Them For Maximum Power (Hammill)
Competition Car Datalogging Manual, The (Templeman)
Custom Air Suspension – How to install air suspension in your road car – on a budget! (Edgar)
Cylinder Heads, How to Build, Modify & Power Tune – Updated & Revised Edition (Burgess & Gollan)
Distributor-type Ignition Systems, How to Build & Power Tune – New 3rd Edition (Hammill)
Fast Road Car, How to Plan and Build – Revised & Updated Colour New Edition (Stapleton)
Holley Carburetors, How to Build & Power Tune – Revised & Updated Edition (Hammill)
Land Rover Discovery, Defender & Range Rover – How to Modify Coil Sprung Models for High Performance & Off-Road Action (Hosier)
Motorsport, Getting Started in (Collins)
Nitrous Oxide High-performance Manual, The (Langfield)
Race & Trackday Driving Techniques (Hornsey)
Retro or classic car for high performance, How to modify your (Stapleton)
Rover V8 Engines, How to Power Tune (Hammill)
Secrets of Speed – Today's techniques for 4-stroke engine blueprinting & tuning (Swager)
SU Carburettor High-performance Manual (Hammill)
Successful Low-Cost Rally Car, How to Build a (Young)
Suzuki 4x4, How to Modify For Serious Off-road Action (Richardson)
V8 Engine, How to Build a Short Block For High Performance (Hammill)
Weber DCOE, & Dellorto DHLA Carburetors, How to Build & Power Tune – 3rd Edition (Hammill)

Workshop Pro Series

Setting up a home car workshop (Edgar)
Car electrical and electronic systems (Edgar)

RAC Handbooks

Caring for your car – How to maintain & service your car (Fry)
Caring for your car's bodywork and interior (Nixon)
Efficient Driver's Handbook, The (Moss)
First aid for your car – Your expert guide to common problems & how to fix them (Collins)
How your car works (Linde)
Selling your car – How to make your car look great and how to sell it fast (Knight)
Simple fixes for your car – How to do small jobs for yourself and save money (Collins)

Enthusiast's Restoration Manual Series

Classic Car Bodywork, How to Restore (Thaddeus)
Classic British Car Electrical Systems (Astley)
Classic Car Electrics (Thaddeus)
Classic Cars, How to Paint (Thaddeus)
How to Restore & Improve Classic Car Suspension, Steering & Wheels (Parish – translator)

Expert Guides

Land Rover Series I-III – Your expert guide to common problems & how to fix them (Thurman)

Essential Buyer's Guide Series

Land Rover Discovery Series I (1989-1998) (Taylor)
Land Rover Discovery Series II (1998-2004) (Taylor)
Land Rover Series I, II & IIA (Thurman)
Land Rover Series III (Thurman)
Range Rover – First Generation models 1970 to 1996 (Taylor)

General

Art Deco and British Car Design (Down)
Automotive A-Z, Lane's Dictionary of Automotive Terms (Lane)
Automotive Mascots (Kay & Springate)
British Cars, The Complete Catalogue of, 1895-1975 (Culshaw & Horrobin)
Car-tastrophes – 80 automotive atrocities from the past 20 years (Honest John, Fowler)
Classic British Car Electrical Systems (Astley)
Competition Car Aerodynamics 3rd Edition (McBeath)
Competition Car Composites A Practical Handbook (Revised 2nd Edition) (McBeath)
Concept Cars, How to illustrate and design – New 2nd Edition (Dewey)
Dorset from the Sea – The Jurassic Coast from Lyme Regis to Old Harry Rocks photographed from its best viewpoint (also Souvenir Edition) (Belasco)
Draw & Paint Cars – How to (Gardiner)
Drive on the Wild Side, A – 20 Extreme Driving Adventures From Around the World (Weaver)
Dune Buggy, Building A – The Essential Manual (Shakespeare)
Dune Buggy Files (Hale)
Dune Buggy Handbook (Hale)
Essential Guide to Driving in Europe, The (Parish)
France: the essential guide for car enthusiasts – 200 things for the car enthusiast to see and do (Parish)
The Good, the Mad and the Ugly ... not to mention Jeremy Clarkson (Dron)
Hillclimbing & Sprinting – The Essential Manual (Short & Wilkinson)
How to Restore & Improve Classic Car Suspension, Steering & Wheels (Parish, translator)
Jaguar from the shop floor (Martin)
Jeep CJ (Ackerson)
Jeep Wrangler (Ackerson)
Land Rover Emergency Vehicles (Taylor)
Land Rover Series III Reborn (Porter)
Land Rover, The Half-ton Military (Cook)
Land Rovers in British Military Service – coil sprung models 1970 to 2007 (Taylor)
Preston Tucker & Others (Linde)
Racing Colours – Motor Racing Compositions 1908-2009 (Newman)
Renewable Energy Home Handbook, The (Porter)
Roads with a View – England's greatest views and how to find them by road (Corfield)
Rover P4 (Bobbitt)
This Day in Automotive History (Corey)
To Boldly Go – twenty six vehicle designs that dared to be different (Hull)
Which Oil? – Choosing the right oils & greases for your antique, vintage, veteran, classic or collector car (Michell)

www.veloce.co.uk

First published in July 2018 by Veloce Publishing Limited, Veloce House, Parkway Farm Business Park, Middle Farm Way, Poundbury, Dorchester DT1 3AR, England. Tel +44 (0)1305 260068 / Fax 01305 250479 / e-mail info@veloce.co.uk / web www.veloce.co.uk or www.velocebooks.com. ISBN: 978-1-787112-44-5 UPC: 6-36847-01244-1.
© 2018 James Taylor and Veloce Publishing. All rights reserved. With the exception of quoting brief passages for the purpose of review, no part of this publication may be recorded, reproduced or transmitted by any means, including photocopying, without the written permission of Veloce Publishing Ltd. Throughout this book logos, model names and designations, etc, have been used for the purposes of identification, illustration and decoration. Such names are the property of the trademark holder as this is not an official publication. Readers with ideas for automotive books, or books on other transport or related hobby subjects, are invited to write to the editorial director of Veloce Publishing at the above address. British Library Cataloguing in Publication Data – A catalogue record for this book is available from the British Library. Typesetting, design and page make-up all by Veloce Publishing Ltd on Apple Mac. Printed in India by Replika Press.

LAND ROVER
Emergency Vehicles

James Taylor

CONTENTS

INTRODUCTION

This book focuses on Land Rover vehicles used by the three main emergency services – Fire, Police and Ambulance – although I am well aware that other services might qualify for the title as well. I am also well aware that the functions of some of these services often overlap, and differ from one country to the next. I should also point out that the book does not pretend to be definitive; it would need a book many times this size to do that. What it does aim to do, however, is to show a representative selection of vehicles over the years.

Land Rovers of one kind or another have been welcomed by the emergency services almost since the day the first one was announced in 1948. Emergencies do not occur conveniently in accessible places, or next to surfaced roads; many of them occur in hard-to-reach places, on farmland or in narrow country lanes. To get to such places, a Land Rover with its four-wheel-drive off-road capability is exactly what the emergency services need.

Demand for specialist vehicles from the fire and ambulance services led Land Rover to sponsor and develop specialist conversions – often quite elaborate ones – during the 1950s. After 1970, the original utility Land Rover was joined by the high-performance Range Rover, and this was a major success with police forces as a motorway patrol vehicle.

The 1960s, 1970s and 1980s were the heyday of Land Rover's involvement with the emergency services. However, the company's re-orientation towards developed markets in the mid-1980s would have a profound effect on that involvement in the longer term. In the mean time, the Discovery provided a useful mid-range model after 1989, as the Range Rover was gradually moved further upmarket until it became too expensive for most emergency-service users.

By the middle of the 1990s, Land Rover's association with the emergency services was inevitably changing, although the Defender remained a favourite because of its versatility and adaptability. However, after the sale of the company to Tata in 2008, Land Rover gradually completed its transformation into a premium maker of luxury vehicles.

As will be apparent from the reduced coverage given to later models in this book, the number of fire, police and ambulance vehicles being ordered from Land Rover is now much smaller than it once was. The reasons are quite clear: Land Rover has been relentlessly pushing all its models upmarket, so increasing purchase costs, and it has been focussing on passenger-carrying luxury models rather than on multi-purpose or commercial vehicles. Nevertheless, the company's official stance is that it remains only too happy to provide fleets of vehicles, as long as the necessary conversion work is done by the buyer.

The pictures and information in this book have been gathered over a period of around 40 years, and very many people have made their contribution, one way or another. Rather than attempt to list them all here, I have credited them as far as possible in the captions to the photographs. In some cases, the identity of a picture's originator has been lost in the mists of time. I have therefore had to fall back on "Author's collection" as the source description; I hope that does not offend anybody.

Meanwhile, I should single out a small number of contributors for special thanks. JLR itself has been very helpful, especially in the person of Roger Crathorne; many pictures reached me with the Richard de Roos collection that became mine about 12 years ago; and I am very much indebted to Paddy Carpenter of PVEC (the Police Vehicle Enthusiasts' Club).

James Taylor
Oxfordshire

Chapter 1

LAND ROVER SERIES I

The Series I models were built between 1948 and 1958. Their evolution fell into three distinct phases: between 1948 and 1953, all models had an 80-inch wheelbase; between 1953 and 1956 there were short-wheelbase (86-inch) and long-wheelbase (107-inch) models; and between 1956 and 1958 the wheelbases were extended to 88 inches and 109 inches, and there was also an anomaly as the long-wheelbase Station Wagon retained the earlier 107-inch dimension.

The engines were always four-cylinders, and there were no diesels before 1956 (except as aftermarket conversions). Up to 1950, the engine was a 50bhp 1.6-litre, which was replaced in 1952 by a 52bhp 2.0-litre. The diesel option from 1956 was a 2.0-litre with the same 52bhp. All Series I models had a four-speed manual gearbox with two-speed transfer box, and the front axle drive could be disconnected for road work after 1950; on earlier models, a freewheel in the drivetrain prevented axle wind-up at road speeds. Suspension was always by semi-elliptic leaf springs, and there were beam axles front and rear, with drum brakes and a separate parking brake acting on the transmission.

FIRE TENDERS

It was obvious from a very early stage that the Land Rover was going to be useful as the basis of a firefighting vehicle because its size and all-terrain capability enabled it to reach fires in places inaccessible to larger, conventional fire appliances. There was a precedent, too: Willys had developed a Fire Jeep derivative of their postwar civilian CJ-2A model for exactly the same purpose.

Rover was not quite so quick off the mark, although the company was certainly experimenting with an 80-inch fire tender by September 1948. However, a production fire tender did not become available until around 1951, and, in the meantime, a number of fire brigades had seen the Land Rover's potential and had made their own adaptations. The earliest known was carried out in Portugal in 1948, and the

The volunteer fire service in Poiares, Portugal could not wait for the factory to make its own Land Rover fire tender. The service bought a standard vehicle in 1948, painted it red and added a ladder rack and siren. It may well have been the very first Land Rover fire engine to enter service anywhere in the world.
(José Almeida)

earliest known in Britain was a batch of four owned by the Derbyshire Fire Service in 1949.

In the beginning, Rover treated the Land Rover fire engine as just another variant of the vehicle, equivalent to the Welder or the Station Wagon. However, it soon became apparent that individual fire brigades wanted features to suit their own needs, not a standardised design. Although Rover persisted with its standardised design for most of the 1950s, handing responsibility for it to the Technical Service Department in 1955, it was clear that a different approach was needed.

When the Special Projects Department was formed in late 1957, to take over from the Technical Service Department and develop its work further, a new approach evolved. Rover planned to farm out the actual conversion work for the fire engine and other adaptations of the Land Rover to specialist companies. The conversions that those companies developed would then be examined by Land Rover engineers and, if they did not affect

(continues on page 13)

The Rover Company was not far behind, and converted one of the pilot-production models to a fire tender. It went through several iterations before being sold to India. (Jaguar Land Rover)

The Rover design evolved, and this 1953 example has a ladder rack and cradles on the front wings to carry full-size fire hoses. The hoses themselves are not fitted in this picture. The equipment lockers at the sides of the load bed have evolved into a simpler design with canvas covers. (Jaguar Land Rover)

A production design was ready by about 1951, and was built by Rover itself. The design included a small first-aid tank, a rear-mounted pump driven from the power take-off, and a first-aid hose. Some examples were fitted with the 'truck cab' roof, as seen on this 1952 model. (Jaguar Land Rover)

Despite the 1955 registration number, this is actually a 1953 80-inch model that was delivered to a Welsh fire brigade. The picture on the left shows how the hoses looked when carried on the bonnet. The close-up pictures show how the first-aid tank was mounted in the load bed, and that the pump was made by Pegson. (Author)

Not every Land Rover fire tender had the full panoply of ladder rack, water tank and pump. This 1955 86-inch model provided fire cover at the Rover factory in Solihull, but seems to have carried little more than extinguishers to tackle small fires. (Jaguar Land Rover)

New in late 1955 or early 1956, this is another 86-inch model, this time with ladder rack and rear-mounted pump. The equipment lockers have been built up with metal covers, although these may not have been original to the vehicle. (John Craddock)

AFF 218 is a 1955 86-inch model that served as factory fire tender at an ICI chemical plant. It carries full-size fire hoses but no ladder-rack. Such variations caused difficulties for Rover, which was not equipped to build multiple minor variations to suit individual requirements. (Author)

John Dickinson Ltd took delivery of three 86-inch Land Rovers to provide fire cover at its Apsley Mills stationery factory. XUR 651 is pictured as it was during the 1960s or 1970s, by which time it had acquired reflective number-plates. (John Dickinson Ltd)

This was XUR 652 when new. There are reels of hose stowed in the side lockers, and the trailer is a Brockhouse of the type sold specifically for the Land Rover. (John Dickinson Ltd)

To complete the set, this picture shows XUR 653 when new. Unlike the other two, it was configured as a hardtop. The enclosed trailer contained breathing apparatus. (John Dickinson Ltd)

This rather wonderful period picture shows an 86-inch fire tender of the Hong Kong Fire Brigade in action. It is probably just a training exercise, but the picture shows very well why a small appliance was needed to deal with fires in the colony's closely-packed high-rise buildings. (Jaguar Land Rover)

the integrity of the host vehicle, they would be granted Land Rover approval. This meant that Rover would honour its standard warranty, and also that the conversions could be ordered through Land Rover dealers, which made the process much more straightforward than it had been.

Meanwhile, the Land Rover itself had evolved, getting bigger each time. The original model with 80-inch wheelbase had grown into an 86-inch in 1953, and then to an 88-inch in 1956.

The 86-inch had been accompanied by a longer derivative with a 107-inch wheelbase, and that in turn had become a 109-inch in 1956. Although long-wheelbase Land Rovers would become favourites for fire appliance conversions in later years, it took a long time for their likely benefits to be appreciated. Rover did not offer one until around 1957, and the development of this 109-inch fire appliance may have been one of the first jobs done by the Special Projects Department. Special Projects also approved a conversion by Fire Armour of London, which

(continues on page 17)

Now in preservation, this 1956 88-inch model was delivered new to a rural fire brigade in New Zealand. The front-mounted hose reel allowed a firefighter to walk ahead of the vehicle as it pumped water to deal with a fire in vegetation or crops. The headlamps were relocated on the wing fronts to suit. The rear steps allowed additional firefighters to ride on the back of the vehicle. (Author)

Quite different from most Series I fire tenders is this one with enclosed rear bodywork. It is not clear which brigade ordered it, or who built the bodywork – it was almost certainly not made by Rover, but by a specialist fire appliance company. (Author's collection)

Fire appliances were much less common on the long-wheelbase Land Rover chassis during the Series I era. The possibilities were, nevertheless, dawning on customers by the time the 109-inch model was introduced in 1956, and this 1957 model was ordered by the West Sussex Fire Brigade. The rear-mounted pump is within the load area, and not exposed as on most short-wheelbase models, but it is not easy to see what other advantages the longer wheelbase was providing. It is not known who did the conversion. (Author's collection)

This fire tender on the 109-inch wheelbase was probably built by Rover, and has a configuration very similar to that of the 88-inch models that the company was making. This time, the fire pump is hung on the rear, and the extra length in the back of the body could have been used for additional equipment such as extinguishers. The registration number is not original to the vehicle, which provided fire cover at the Winfrith nuclear power station in Dorset. (Author)

Above: This 109-inch model has a very similar configuration to the Winfrith vehicle, and served its time on the Woomera rocket range in Australia. It was pictured in preservation. **Right:** The Rover-built fire appliances normally came with red upholstery, and were painted red inside the cab and under the bonnet. This is the cab of the ex-Woomera 109. (Wayne Ellard)

This 109 fire tender provided cover at the Massey Ferguson tractor plant in Sunshine, Victoria, New South Wales. The body would appear to have been built locally. (Author's collection)

16

had designed a model called the Hi-Fog type, by early 1957. However, this remained rare.

POLICE VEHICLES

The value of the Land Rover as a police vehicle became apparent outside Britain long before British police forces decided to buy any. For police services in Africa and the Middle East, it was an ideal vehicle because its rugged build and cross-country ability allowed it to survive in terrain that defeated ordinary cars.

By 1956, a Land Rover promotional brochure listed 26 overseas countries where Land Rovers were in police use, which was an impressive total. That list was as follows:

Angola	Gold Coast	Saudi Arabia
Bahrain	Hong Kong	Tanganyika
Belgium	Indo-China	Thailand
Brazil	Iran	Trinidad
Canada (RCMP)	Kenya	Tunisia
Ceylon	Lebanon	Turkey
Ecuador	Martinique	Uganda
Ethiopia	Mauritius	Uruguay
French West Africa	Nigeria	

Other countries would join the list later, including Cyprus and Spain.

The large canvas bag on the roof of this Belgian 80-inch model appears to conceal a public-address system, and the officer in the passenger seat holds a microphone that is presumably connected to it. (Gendarmerie Nationale)

In Britain, few police forces seem to have known what to make of the Land Rover. Its poor road performance was almost certainly an inhibiting factor in police purchase decisions. However, there certainly were some short-wheelbase models in police service in some parts of the country by the middle of the 1950s.

An early police user of Land Rovers was the Belgian Gendarmerie. These examples are 80-inch models that appear to date from around 1952, and would have been painted dark blue. Of interest is that the Gendarmerie fitted them with flashing turn signals; semaphore arms were still the standard factory option. (Gendarmerie Nationale)

Apparently dating from the same period, this Gendarmerie Land Rover is pictured during a parade, suitably smartened up with stylish whitewall tyres. The Gendarmerie was a paramilitary organisation until 1992, and the four officers seated in the rear have their rifles on display. (Gendarmerie Nationale)

The Liverpool City Police force was an early user of Land Rovers in Britain. This is a 1956 86-inch model in use on a night patrol. (Merseyside Police)

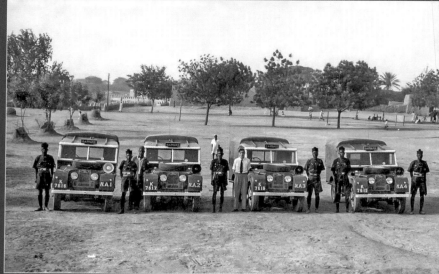

These four vehicles belonged to the police force in one of Britain's African colonies, and are fairly typical of their type. Note that all of them carry two-way radios with an aerial mounted on the cab roof. (Jaguar Land Rover)

Spain's Policia Armada used Land Rovers from around 1957, and this is an early 88-inch model. The livery was mid-grey and the force emblem on the door was black. All the Land Rovers visible in this picture have been smartened up for a parade with whitewall tyres. (Author's collection)

Above and right: This 107-inch model belonged to the Hong Kong Police. It was equipped with a public-address system, and those seated in the back were protected by mesh guards and a solid roof that contained vision panels. (Jaguar Land Rover)

Left: Another overseas police force that joined the ranks of Land Rover users towards the end of the Series I era was the Cyprus Police. At this stage, it was a paramilitary force that belonged to the British Colonial Government. These vehicles are 88-inch models. (Pip Brown)

AMBULANCES

There was little doubt that the short-wheelbase Land Rover was too small to work as an ambulance, and although there were several field conversions by the military in various countries, the stretcher always ended up hanging off the back of the vehicle.

The first Land Rover ambulance produced in any volume was probably the one that the RAF ordered from commercial body builder Bonallack in 1955. These were for its Mountain Rescue service, originally set up to rescue downed pilots, but in practice increasingly playing a role in civilian mountain rescue operations as well. The bodies were built on 107-inch Station Wagon chassis, which had outrigged rear springs that reduced body roll. (Tank Museum/FVRDE)

None of that prevented a determined chief ambulance officer in Staffordshire from having a special ambulance body built on an 80-inch chassis. No pictures of this have been found except for a small one published in *Commercial Motor* magazine at the time. The body was built by Reeve & Kenning in Pilsbury, near Chesterfield. It appears that the front passenger seat may have been removed so that a stretcher could be made to fit within the body. However, this experiment probably remained unique.

It was not until the long-wheelbase Land Rover became available that ambulance builders began to exploit the vehicle's possibilities. In 1955, commercial body builder Bonallack & Sons at Basildon in Essex secured a contract

Land Rovers tended to go where the British had colonial influence. This large line-up of long-wheelbase models (it is impossible to tell whether they are 107s or 109s) belonged to the Malayan police. (Jaguar Land Rover)

Pilchers of Merton was groping its way towards an ambulance design on the long-wheelbase chassis. This one is essentially a truck cab pick-up with a tall hardtop that incorporates frosted windows. Whether it was a full ambulance or more of a mobile dispensary is impossible to tell. (Pilcher-Greene)

from the War Department to build a special Mountain Rescue ambulance on the 107-inch Station Wagon chassis – chosen in preference to the standard chassis because of its improved resistance to cornering roll from springs mounted further outboard. However, the Bonallack ambulance was never commercialised, and the military ones probably remained the only examples ever built.

The earliest known civilian ambulance conversion, nevertheless, also dates from 1955. It was built on a 107-inch chassis and came from Herbert Lomas, an ambulance specialist based at Handforth near Wilmslow in Cheshire. This vehicle had a fully coachbuilt body, and was probably evaluated by the Technical Service Department at Rover. The following year a similar vehicle (possibly the same one) was in service with the Civil Defence organisation. It carried a single stretcher on the left, and three seated patients on the right.

Pilchers of Merton was next with an ambulance, although the company had already been building mobile dispensaries for rural areas, and there may have been ambulance versions of those. However, the Pilchers ambulance was created more simply than the Lomas type, by adding a tall hardtop to a pick-up body. It is not clear how well this sold.

By early 1957, Pilchers had an ambulance body on the long-wheelbase Land Rover chassis. It was still little more than a tall hardtop fitted to a standard 107-inch truck cab, although there were proper rear doors for patient access, and the interior was arranged to carry both seated patients and a stretcher. (Pilcher-Greene)

Chapter 2

SERIES II & SERIES IIA

SERIES II

The Series II Land Rover was introduced in April 1958, with 88-inch and 109-inch wheelbases as before. The date was exactly 10 years after the introduction of the first Land Rover, but the real reason for the arrival of the Series II was the threat of competition from the new Austin Gipsy. In practice, the Gipsy never did present much of a threat, but the changes to the Land Rover were nevertheless important.

Mechanical changes centred on a new and much more powerful 2286cc OHV four-cylinder petrol engine, which shared the same basic layout as the 2052cc diesel that remained available. In practice, very early 88-inch Series II models retained the old 2-litre petrol engine. Much more obvious, though, was the new body styling, with barrel-sides to cover wider-track axles, a sill panel to conceal the underpinnings, and a particularly neat truck cab option. This basic styling was so successful that it would continue with only minor changes until 2016 – a total of 58 years.

The Land Rover Fire Tender on the early Series II 88 was supplied by the factory, but was almost certainly built by Carmichael. It had many details in common with that company's later Redwing FT/1 model. (Jaguar Land Rover)

Carmichael's FT/5 had enclosed bodywork with a GRP roof. This 1959 example was new to a paper manufacturer, where it became the factory fire engine. An enclosed body was ideal when a vehicle was stored in the open, and there was a risk of weather damage to, or theft of, the firefighting equipment. (Author)

wheelbase chassis. An additional support frame above the chassis allowed a 30cwt (3360lb, 1524kg) payload, and larger 9.00 x 16 tyres were specified, together with altered transfer box gearing.

The Series IIA Forward Control was introduced in 1962, and came with the existing four-cylinder petrol and diesel engines, or with an 83bhp version of the Rover 2.6-litre six-cylinder saloon car engine that was for export only. Without the six-cylinder engine, it was always a cumbersome vehicle, and even with it was not much liked. Nevertheless, it provided the necessary space for some types of specialist conversion.

The Series IIB Forward Control brought much-needed improvements in 1966. This had wider-track, heavy-duty axles (also available optionally on the final IIA models), and minor chassis adjustments that led to a 110-inch wheelbase. They also had changed gearing and improved controls, and the six-cylinder engine now became available in Britain. Headlamps on the 110-inch Forward Control were mounted lower down, to meet regulations in some export markets, although some late Series IIAs had been modified to this standard, and for the same reason.

All the Forward Control models were slow sellers, and the last Series IIB types were built in 1972.

Series IIA

The Series IIA, introduced in 1961, was a logical evolution of the Series II, and the only important specification change was to a 2286cc version of the diesel engine. From 1966, the 83bhp 2.6-litre six-cylinder petrol engine from the Forward Control models (see below) became available alongside the 2.25-litre four-cylinder petrol and diesel types. Then, in April 1969, the headlights were recessed into the wing fronts to meet new legislation in some export markets; as a temporary measure, those markets had received models with the headlamps mounted on the wing fronts in early 1969.

From June 1969, the existing 88-inch and 109-inch models were joined by a heavy-duty One Ton version of the 109. This had the lower transfer box gearing and 9.00 x 16 tyres pioneered on the Forward Control models.

The Series IIA models went out of production in mid-1971 and were replaced by Series III types. Some of the last Series IIAs had the stronger rear axle, and all-synchromesh gearbox designed for the Series IIIs.

Forward Control

By moving the cab ahead of the engine, Rover engineers created room for a longer rear body on the 109-inch

Fire vehicles

Land Rover fire tenders became big business during the 1960s. The first couple of years of the Series II models were a little hesitant, as Rover managed the transition from building its own fire tenders to farming out the business to approved converters, but thereafter the number of different conversions multiplied. Not only were the 88-inch and 109-inch models turned into fire tenders, but so too was the new Forward Control that became available in 1962. As export orders increased, probably the majority of all Land Rover fire tenders built in this period were sold outside Britain.

At the start of the Series II period, only Carmichael had Land Rover Approval for its fire tenders, but by November 1959 approval had also been granted to Fire Armour. The Carmichael company, which used the Redwing brand name, remained resolutely independent right through the 1960s and for many years after that, but Fire Armour was absorbed by the George Angus Group, and briefly became Angus Fire Armour before merging with HCB Engineering in 1963 to become HCB-Angus. HCB-Angus went on to become a major name in the Land Rover fire tender business.

It was probably in 1965 that Land Rover appointed a third approved fire tender converter. This was Sun Engineering, which was bought out by Pyrene in the later 1960s; as a result, the Sun conversions are relatively little known. From about 1969, there were also fire appliances from Branbridge. So by the end of Series IIA production in 1971, Land Rover fire tenders on the Series IIA 88 and 109 chassis were available from four British specialists: Branbridge, Carmichael, HCB-Angus, and Pyrene.

Not every Land Rover fire appliance was actually a formal conversion by a specialist company. Some fire brigades both in Britain and overseas created their own conversions, especially when the Land Rover was to be used as an equipment carrier and did not require a fire pump or water tank. The host vehicle was usually a 109 hardtop or Station Wagon, although there were also a few based on 88s.

FORWARD CONTROL MODELS
Different converters became involved with the Forward Control models. The Series IIA (109-inch) model became popular with volunteer fire brigades in the mountain villages of Austria and Switzerland, because it could be configured to carry a number of firefighters, as well as firefighting equipment. The two major builders of these were Rosenbauer

The Snowy Mountains Hydro-Electric Authority in Australia bought several Fire Armour Firefly tenders on 109 chassis. This 1960 Series II was pictured in preservation, and shows the characteristic lines of the back body. (Wayne Ellard)

This HCB-Angus appliance on an early Series IIA was designed for rural firefighting duties. The body configuration, with hose reels let into sunken sections in the body sides, was similar to the Hi-Fog airfield fire appliance that had been built by Fire Armour, one of the companies that had become part of HCB-Angus. (HCB-Angus)

Another example of an enclosed body, this time with built-in lockers. This 1961 Series IIA 109 was built by Fire Armour and belonged to the Central Region Fire Brigade in Scotland. It served at a volunteer fire station until the late 1980s, and is now in preservation. (Archie McKinnon)

at Linz in Austria, and Bücher in the German town of Rothenburg, just over the Swiss border. A conversion is also known from De Dion Bouton in France. Most of these continental European conversions probably had the six-cylinder engine, which was readily available for export, but could not be had in Britain.

After the Series IIB (110-inch) Forward Control model arrived in 1966, and the six-cylinder engine option became available on the home market, British fire brigades took an interest. So Carmichael, HCB-Angus, and Merryweather all developed conversions. The volunteer brigades in the Alpine regions of southern Europe continued to take locally-built conversions, and the Rosenbauer conversions were joined after 1968 by a distinctive and more modern-looking conversion by Willi Müller of Romanshorn in Switzerland. Kronenburg at Hedel in the Netherlands also built fire tenders on the later Forward Control chassis.

It was quite common for Land Rover fire engines to tow a separate water tank. Their role was first-aid firefighting while the larger appliances reached the scene of the incident. This is an early 1960s Series IIA Redwing (probably an FT/2) by Carmichael. The tropical roof on the truck cab suggests that this example was destined for export. (Carmichael)

Sun Engineering had become a fire tender builder by the middle of the 1960s, and this 109 displays the maker's name on the front wing. (Jaguar Land Rover)

Some fire brigades made their own adaptations, and this Dutch example was based on a 109 Station Wagon. It has the 'bugeye' headlamp configuration sold in some European countries in late 1968 and early 1969 to meet new lighting regulations. (Jan Pieper)

This late Series IIA was built by Arnolds (Branbridges) of East Peckham in Kent, and was pictured providing fire cover at a preserved railway line. It was usually known as a Peckham type. Arnolds later became Branbridge, which was subsequently taken over by Pilcher-Greene. (Author)

The Sun Engineering designs passed to Pyrene in the late 1960s, but the Sun brand was still in use when this late Series IIA was built in 1969. (Author)

Rosenbauer built the body on this Series IIA 109 Forward Control for a volunteer fire brigade in the Alpine region. The front section was designed to carry additional crew members, while firefighting equipment was carried in the back and on the roof. This is the headlamp configuration associated with the Series IIA models. The lamps were mounted lower on the Series IIB Forward Control, and also on some late Series IIA types for continental Europe. (Helmuth Guss)

Although it carries a Parisian number-plate, this French Series IIA Forward Control was almost certainly intended for forest firefighting duties in the south of the country. It was built by De Dion Bouton, whose name is emblazoned on the nose. (Jaguar Land Rover)

This is another interpretation of the Alpine volunteer brigade requirements, by Bücher. The back body has a crew compartment at the front and carries firefighting equipment in the rear. Just visible is a ladder on the roof. (Author)

Once the six-cylinder engine became available for British buyers in the Series IIB 110 Forward Control, British specialists developed fire appliance versions. This one dates from 1972, and is a very late example of a Carmichael FT/7, which served as a factory fire tender for the Rover Company. (Author)

The HCB-Angus design on the Series IIB Forward Control was broadly similar to the Carmichael type. This 1969 example was part of the large order by the British Ministry of Defence for domestic fire tenders; when sold into civilian hands and re-registered, it served with a helicopter company. (Author)

Rosenbauer in Austria continued with the same design of body on Series IIB Forward Controls. A close look reveals only minor differences between this one and the Series IIA illustrated. (Helmuth Guss)

FORWARD-CONTROL CONVERSIONS

There were also fire appliances based on standard Land Rover chassis, that had been converted to a forward-control layout. The most numerous of these was Carmichael's Redwing FT/6, of which the prototype was built in 1961 on a Series II, but production models were Series IIA types. The advantage of these conversions was that they offered extra space in the body for either additional firefighters or additional equipment, while

This strikingly modern-looking design on the Series IIB chassis came from Willi Müller of Romanshorn in Switzerland. New in 1968, it was much liked, and when the Forward Control ceased production in 1972, the design was later taken on by Wilhelm Marte, who converted several standard Series III 109 chassis to forward control to take it. (Author's collection)

Alfred Miles was better known for its work in the aircraft industry, but in 1960 it developed a forward-control conversion of the Series II 88 chassis with fire tender body. This is the prototype, pictured awaiting restoration, which served on a local industrial estate in Gloucestershire. (Author)

There were perhaps no more than two 'production' Alfred Miles 88 fire tenders, both on Series IIA 88 chassis, and each slightly different from the other. This 1962 example belonged to the Baker Perkins factory fire brigade. (Robin Lafosse)

Pictured in preservation, this is a Carmichael FT/6, the company's forward-control conversion based on a 109-inch chassis. The driving position was moved forward onto an extension welded to the front of the chassis to create more room in the body, which made clever use of standard Land Rover panels along with some new ones. This example was new in 1964 to the Army Fire Service, where it served as a domestic tender, but later served with a factory fire brigade. Inset: The standard Land Rover bulkhead was relocated further back in the FT/6, to create a stiffening member in the middle of the body. Carmichael provided the red seats as standard. (Author)

retaining the low profile of the normal-control Land Rover. Alfred Miles, a Gloucestershire company better known for its work in the aircraft industry, also created forward-control fire tenders from a very small number of 88-inch Land Rovers.

POLICE VEHICLES

Even though police forces in many overseas countries had recognised the Land Rover as exactly the vehicle they needed, especially for rural policing duties, British forces in general were not so impressed. Rapid response is often a requirement of police work, and the Series II and Series IIA Land Rovers were never rapid vehicles.

Nevertheless, Land Rovers were used by several British police forces during the 1960s in special roles. A Land Rover was ideal for towing a mobile incident room, for removing accident-damaged or illegally parked vehicles, or to act as the platform for a warning sign that needed to be seen from as far away as possible.

As a result, the Land Rovers that entered police service were, for the most part, standard production models. The purchasing force would make any necessary modifications in its own workshops, adding signs, lights, bells, sirens, equipment racks, and so on. There were, though, a few police vehicles that were very specially modified, and some are illustrated among the pictures that follow.

The Liverpool City Police were already using Land Rovers for certain types of patrol work by the time the Series II models became available. These pictures show a 1958 88-inch model with hardtop bodywork. The paintwork was almost certainly dark blue. There were very few modifications from standard, although a ladder was carried in a rack on the roof. It was probably used to aid access to buildings where suspicious activity had been detected. (Merseyside Police)

Also in Liverpool, the Mersey Tunnel Police Authority used specially adapted 88-inch Land Rovers to deal with incidents in the tunnel, and to keep traffic moving. The first vehicles had an all-over red livery (as immortalised by the famous Dinky Toys model), but later ones had the brown and cream livery seen on these two 1961 deliveries. (Mersey Tunnel Authority)

Elsewhere in Britain, the value of a Land Rover to police forces was generally limited. The Kent County Constabulary had this 1963 109-inch Series IIA truck cab model on the fleet, but it was probably used mainly for towing duties, such as that pictured here. The large caravan is actually a mobile incident command unit. (Kent Police Museum)

Above: The covered back body on the Mersey Tunnel police vehicles carried equipment for dealing with incidents. Seen here on a 1962 example are extinguishers and a coal scuttle, which would be used to help clear spillages. (Mersey Tunnel Authority)

Above: Outside Britain, the Land Rover was more of a police favourite. In the 1960s, the Hong Kong Police had a number of 109-inch Station Wagons which did duty both as routine transport for officers and for patrol work. Painted dark grey, they had white roofs and the force crest on each rear door. This picture was probably taken during a period of riots in 1967, as all the vehicles visible have metal window grilles (which were not standard), and the officer on the right is wearing riot gear with a metal helmet. The vehicle itself probably dates from 1965. (PVEC)

Right: This 1968 Series IIA 109-inch hardtop belonged to London's Metropolitan Police. By this stage, police vehicles were increasingly entering service in white, which was much more easily visible than the traditional dark blues and blacks. That such vehicles were used for specialist roles is clear from what this one is doing – removing a crashed car from the scene of the accident. (Metropolitan Police)

Above left: The adapted caravan that the Kent force used was later replaced by a much larger mobile incident command unit, which, in this case, had to be demounted from its wheels before use. The towing vehicle may well be the very same Land Rover. (Kent Police Museum)

Above right: The equipment carried in this Metropolitan Police 109-inch hardtop reveals its use in dealing with traffic incidents. There are cones, warning signs, flashing beacons, and a fire extinguisher. (Metropolitan Police)

Left: This is another Metropolitan Police 109 hardtop, this time dating from 1966. Again the specialist use is clear: the Land Rover has been chosen to carry a warning sign on its roof because it is a tall vehicle, and the sign will be visible from some distance away. (Metropolitan Police)

In the 1960s, the Avon & Somerset Police were responsible for cliff rescue work in the force area, a task which has since been passed on to an independent specialist team. This remarkable vehicle was based on a late Series IIA 109 that was fitted with a winch and jib for lowering rescuers to the scene of an incident and bringing both them and the victims back up again.
(Avon & Somerset Police)

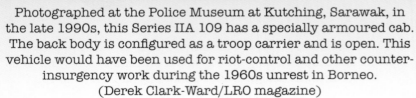

Photographed at the Police Museum at Kutching, Sarawak, in the late 1990s, this Series IIA 109 has a specially armoured cab. The back body is configured as a troop carrier and is open. This vehicle would have been used for riot-control and other counter-insurgency work during the 1960s unrest in Borneo.
(Derek Clark-Ward/LRO magazine)

Also dating from the period of communist insurgency in Borneo, is this fully armoured Series IIA 109. The chassis is an Australian-assembled example with the six-cylinder engine, and the vehicle was again on display in the late 1990s at the Police Museum at Kutching, Sarawak.
(Derek Clark-Ward/LRO magazine)

AMBULANCE CONVERSIONS

It was the 109-inch Land Rover that formed the basis of ambulance conversions during the Series II and Series IIA period. At the end of the 1950s, Land Rover granted its approval to several designs from Pilchers, who had already been building ambulances and mobile dispensaries on long-wheelbase Series I chassis. By the end of 1958, there was also at least one design from established ambulance specialists, Herbert Lomas. Lomas went on to gain Land Rover Approval for its ambulance conversions, although that formal approval seems not to have been granted before the middle of the 1960s.

Ambulance types ranged from simple designs which added a hardtop to a pick-up body, through more elaborate conversions of Station Wagons, and up to the most expensive fully coachbuilt designs, with aluminium panelling on wooden frames. The coachbuilt designs were typically capable of carrying two stretchers, but customer demand led to four-stretcher versions as well, and during the 1960s GRP bodies on metal frames began to provide a less expensive way of providing an ambulance with acceptable interior proportions. The coachbuilt types gradually disappeared, and had become uncommon by the end of the decade.

The Royal Ulster Constabulary had a very specific problem with civil unrest, and in tandem with Belfast engineering works, Short Brothers & Harland, it designed an armoured Land Rover to deal with this. Although the Shorland Armoured Car was initially intended as a police vehicle, Shorts found a ready market for it among military and paramilitary forces outside the UK. The RUC took on its first Shorland in 1966, which was based on an uprated Series IIA chassis. Initially used for border patrol work, the RUC Shorlands later saw service within the city of Belfast. After a review of policing in the province, the Shorlands were later handed over to the Ulster Defence Regiment; the second photograph shows two of them in UDR service, re-registered with military plates. (Shorts)

The most basic type of ambulance was created by adding a special hardtop to a long-wheelbase truck cab model. This was the 'standard' design from Pilchers by the early 1960s. (Pilcher-Greene)

In Britain, a Land Rover ambulance would typically be used on large factory sites, or in rural areas where size and four-wheel drive were factors in gaining access to incidents. Nevertheless, most conversions probably went overseas, especially to countries where roads were poor, and access to medical care might entail quite long journeys. For that reason, relatively few Land Rover ambulances from this period have survived.

It was quite common for Land Rovers of all types to be pressed into service as ambulances when the need arose. These three were operated by a charity at Joyramkura in Bangladesh. All are Series IIA types, and those nearest and furthest from the camera are both Station Wagons. The full extent of their ambulance 'conversion' is not clear, but it may not have extended beyond the Ambulance sign on the roof. The vehicle in the centre is a late (post-1969) Series IIA window hardtop. (Jaguar Land Rover)

This was one way of turning a Station Wagon into an ambulance; there was just room for a stretcher behind each front seat. The rear side panel has been removed to show the interior layout of this Invercarron conversion, made at Stonehaven in Scotland. By mid-1966, Invercarron also offered a budget conversion, with a special hardtop on a 109 truck cab, and an interior fitted with stretchers and seats to suit the customer's wishes. (Author's collection)

The 'standard' conversion from Pilchers also formed the basis of a mobile veterinary clinic. In this case, the GRP roof was produced without windows, and the interior of the body provided an operating theatre. (Jaguar Land Rover)

36

Among the earliest coachbuilt ambulance designs was this one by Herbert Lomas Ltd, from Handforth, near Wilmslow in Cheshire. The example pictured is believed to be the first of its kind, and was built towards the end of 1958 on a Series II 109 chassis for Denbighshire County Council.
(Herbert Lomas Ltd, via Alan Hammond)

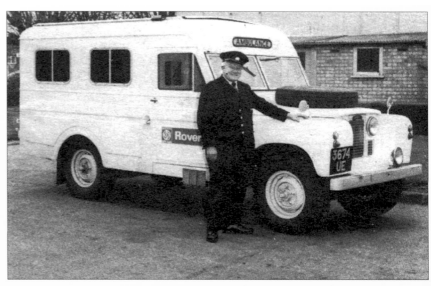

This early example of the coachbuilt Pilchers body was built in 1960 on a Series II chassis, and became the works ambulance at Rover's Acocks Green plant. It is pictured in the 1970s – now wearing a British Leyland logo on the door – on the retirement of its long-term driver. (Jaguar Land Rover)

This handsome vehicle was Pilchers' interpretation of the coachbuilt ambulance. The stylish panelwork was in aluminium alloy, and those pressings in the side sections were primarily designed to strengthen the structure and prevent drumming. Pilchers initially called it the Land Rover Cross-Country Ambulance, and it was normally configured to take two stretchers. This example is on a left-hand-drive Series IIA 109 chassis. (Pilcher-Greene)

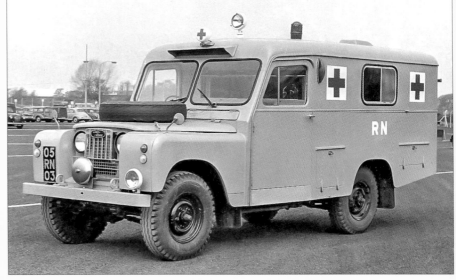

Still coachbuilt, this early 1960s design by Lomas was adopted by the Royal Navy for a fleet of ambulances used at its shore stations. Lomas knew it as the F/M type. The special military-pattern grille protector was normally used only on radio vehicles with a 24-volt electrical system. Some, and perhaps all, of these ambulances were painted yellow. (Jaguar Land Rover)

Herbert Lomas offered several different coachbuilt ambulance bodies. This was the J/C type, which was the least expensive of them, and featured aluminium panels on a wooden frame. This is a very late example of the type, registered in 1967.
(Author's collection)

These two pictures show the Pilchers Type J or 'Junior' ambulance, which had a body made from GRP. The one on trade plates dates from the mid-1960s, and the other from 1969, and it is easy to see how the design had evolved in the two or three years between the two vehicles.
(Pilcher-Greene)

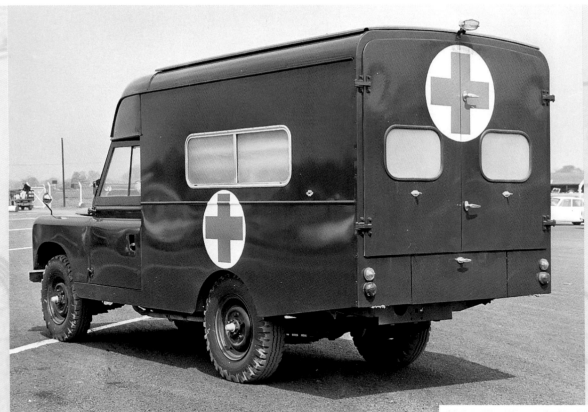

This was yet another design from Pilchers, with a four-stretcher metal-panelled body that had a much simpler design than the company's top-model coachbuilt ambulance. It was available by 1964, and was clearly intended for military use. Note how the body overhangs the rear chassis crossmember by several inches to provide valuable additional interior space. (Pilcher-Greene)

Pilchers gave their designs identifying numbers in the later 1960s, and this was number 7489-S3. By this stage, it had become their 'standard' design and was available with either two or four stretchers. Although made of GRP, it now incorporated its own cab section instead of using standard Land Rover panels. (Pilcher-Greene)

As some earlier pictures make clear, the Carmichael FT/6 forward control conversion was primarily intended as a fire tender. However, a very small number of these vehicles received other types of bodywork, and this 1964 example was probably the only one ever built as an ambulance. There is no indication of who built the body, but as owners Denbighshire County Council are known to have favoured Herbert Lomas (see picture on page 37), and that company was located not far away in Cheshire, there is a good chance that this body was one of theirs. (Alan Hammond)

This style of ambulance body was standardised for British military purchases. The first contract went to Mickleover in 1959, and the vehicles were based on Series II 109s. These had a two-stretcher design. Later deliveries, like this one, were built to the same design by Marshall of Cambridge, and after about 1964 were configured to carry four stretchers. The same ambulance body was also used on Series III models. (Author)

This was the interior of the Marshall military ambulance in four-stretcher form. The upper stretcher rack could be folded against the side wall so that the lower position could carry three seated casualties. (Author)

The Australian military used a very different ambulance, built in Australia to their own design. (Stephen Stansfield)

Chapter 3
SERIES III

The Series III Land Rover was introduced in autumn 1971 and was really a further developed Series IIA. The major mechanical improvements were an all-synchromesh gearbox (actually seen on some late Series IIAs) and a stronger rear axle. The Series IIIs were recognisable by their new one-piece moulded grille in ABS plastic, flat hinges for all side doors, and (for most markets) heater intake on the passenger's side front wing. On the inside, they came with a new black plastic dashboard that located the instruments directly in front of the driver.

As before, there were 88-inch and 109-inch chassis sizes, with uprated One Ton versions of the 109-inch chassis until 1977. In the beginning, the engines were the same 77bhp 2.25-litre petrol and 62bhp 2.25-litre diesel four-cylinders as had powered the Series IIAs, together with the same 83bhp 2.6-litre six-cylinder for the 109-inch models only.

Engine changes followed at the turn of the decade. First of all, the six-cylinder was replaced by a 91bhp version of the 3.5-litre V8 in early 1979, although British sales were delayed until autumn 1980. The V8 models had a permanent four-wheel drive system, were visually distinguished by a flush front, and were known as Stage 1 V8 types. In 1980, the two four-cylinder engines were re-engineered with five main bearings, and were now marketed as 2.3-litre types, although they retained their original 2286cc swept volume.

The final Series III change of importance to the emergency-vehicle market came in spring 1982, when a new High-Capacity Pick-Up (HCPU) back body was offered, with the option of an uprated 1.3-tonne payload.

The coil-sprung One Ten models, introduced in April 1983, gradually replaced the Series III 109s. First to go were the Stage 1 V8s, in 1983, but the 88s and four-cylinder 109s continued into 1985, mainly to fulfil outstanding overseas orders.

FIRE APPLIANCES

As the Series III entered production, four specialist fire

appliance companies had Land Rover approval. These were Branbridge, Carmichael, HCB-Angus, and Pyrene. All had offered similar conversions on the Series IIA chassis, and all of them continued to sell their conversions in quantity.

As before, the majority of all conversions went to overseas customers.

These companies were joined by two more during the lifetime

Carmichael's Redwing FT/5 still looked much the same in 1980 as it had done 20 years earlier. This one belonged to an ICI factory fire brigade. By this time, the manufacturer was known as Carmichael Fire, and was a division of the company now called Carmichael Fire and Bulk Ltd. (Roger Conway)

This was a more straightforward conversion by HCB-Angus, based on a 109 hardtop, and again used by a factory fire brigade, in this case John Dickinson Stationery at Apsley. The special trailer contained breathing apparatus. (John Dickinson Ltd)

of the Series III. The fifth company in the market was Dennis Eagle Ltd, which began offering Land Rover-based appliances in about 1977; and the sixth was Angloco Ltd, about a year later.

There were two further changes among these manufacturers. Pyrene was bought by Chubb in the early 1970s, becoming Pyrene Chubb Fire Security Ltd, although it was usually known simply as Chubb. Branbridge was bought out by Pilcher Greene some time around 1980. In both cases, the earlier designs were continued under the new brand names. By the end of the Series III era, Land Rover itself was listing fire appliance conversions only by Angus, Carmichael and Chubb, although Angloco was still offering its conversions as well.

There were also some purpose-built forward-control fire tender conversions, built by Bates of Evesham, on the Series III 109 chassis.

As was the case during the Series II and Series IIA period, some end users bypassed the specialist converters and created their own fire support vehicles. Typically, these were again based on 109 hardtops or Station Wagons, although there were also some on the 88-inch chassis.

Outside the UK, several companies built Series III fire tenders to meet local requirements. In Austria, specialists Rosenbauer of Leonding built some on 109 chassis, and Theodor Marte of Wolfurt converted some 109s to forward control configuration, and bodied them with a design developed in the late 1960s for the Series IIB Forward Control models by Willi Müller of Romanshorn in Switzerland.

This early Series III 109 by HCB-Angus originally belonged to a hospital fire brigade, whose name was painted on the red panels above the unpainted back body. (Author)

This late 1970s appliance by HCB-Angus was pictured giving a demonstration of its pumping skills. By this time, the roller shutters in the back body had been replaced by what were known as 'fish-fryer' hinged panels, and HCB-Angus had adopted the brand name of Firestrike for its Land Rover appliances. (Jaguar Land Rover)

Branbridge made its mark with a special low-profile fire tender that was designed to operate in areas with restricted height, such as multi-storey car parks. The large front bumper assembly actually contained an auxiliary water tank. Some examples of this type had two doors on the passenger side, but just one on the driver's side, to allow space for equipment where the fourth door would otherwise have been. (Left: Jaguar Land Rover; Right: Author)

The Branbridge designs were taken over by Pilcher Greene and remained available. This one is on a Series III Stage 1 V8 chassis from around 1980. (Jaguar Land Rover)

Above and below: Angloco was based in Batley, Yorkshire, and was a latecomer to the Land Rover fire appliance business. The left-hand drive Series III 109 was known as a 450LRX type. It dates from around 1980 and was obviously destined for an overseas customer. (Angloco)

After Eagle of Warwick was absorbed into the Dennis group, Dennis Eagle entered the market with this low-cost appliance based on a 109. Costs were contained by the use of a portable fire pump driven by its own small petrol engine, instead of a PTO-driven pump. (Dennis Eagle)

Another latecomer to the market was VF Specialist Vehicles. This 1980 model has a heavy-duty specification with 9.00 x 16 tyres, and belonged to a works fire brigade in Peterborough. (Author)

The Austrian firm of Rosenbauer continued to convert Land Rovers to fire appliances during the Series III era, and this Station Wagon was used by a Norwegian brigade. (Author's collection)

These two views show a Carmichael FT/6 forward control conversion at two stages in its life. The front view shows it with its second owner, a factory fire brigade, and the rear view shows it before delivery to its first owner, a brigade in Gwynedd, Wales. From about 1976, this angular body made largely from GRP replaced the earlier FT/6 type with bulbous snout, which is illustrated in the chapter on Series IIA fire conversions. (Left: Gordon Smith; Right: Carmichael)

In the mid-1970s, Bates of Evesham built a number of special conversions for the Northern Ireland Fire Service. They were six-cylinder 109s, converted to forward-control layout and fitted with special bodywork. The rear view of one under renovation shows how tall and narrow the bodywork was. (Author)

VF Specialist Vehicles produced this six-wheel appliance to provide fire cover for a helicopter operator in 1983. The base vehicle was a 109-inch Stage 1 V8. (Nick Dimbleby)

POLICE

Sales of Land Rover products to British police forces improved dramatically during the 1970s, thanks to the introduction of the Range Rover at the start of the decade. However, the new model did not eat into traditional sales to any noticeable extent, because it was adopted for quite different purposes. So, sales of long-wheelbase hardtops and the occasional Station Wagon continued during the Series III era. As before, individual forces generally made modifications in their

The majority of Land Rovers sold to police forces in Britain by the time o the Series III were 109-inch hardtop models. So the demonstrator vehicle had that specification. Here it is in a publicity photograph from 1971. The police livery was deliberately generic, and reflects concerns of the time that vehicles needed to be more visible from behind in poor light conditions – which is why the rear end is painted red. (Jaguar Land Rover)

Nevertheless, 109 hardtops were not the only Land Rovers taken on by police forces in Britain. This is a 109 Station Wagon that was new to the Metropolitan Police in 1977, and was pictured assisting in the smooth passage across London's roads of an oversized load. Although there is a traditional bell on the front bumper, there are also loud-hailers on the roof to act as a public-address system when the occasion warranted it. (Metropolitan Police)

The bell is still present on this 1978 Metropolitan Police 109 hardtop. Additional lights on the roof and front bumper reflect changing demands and conditions, and this vehicle is obviously equipped with a two-way radio. It also has large pusher bars on the front bumper, designed to allow the Land Rover to push obstructions – such as stranded vehicles – out of the way. The chromed wing mirrors were added to suit police requirements, and gave a much wider field of vision than the standard Land Rover type. (Metropolitan Police)

Just a year later, this 109 hardtop had very much the same specification, although in this case it does not have its spare wheel mounted on the bonnet. Again, this one was used by London's Metropolitan Police. (Metropolitan Police)

These two former Metropolitan Police hardtops were of a very different type. They were armoured vehicles, based on the heavy-duty One Ton 109 chassis, and were bought as a response to increases in the terrorist threat in the late 1970s. AYL 255T was originally white with a yellow roof, and spent some time stationed at London's Heathrow Airport. It was also used by police during the hostage-taking incident at the Iranian Embassy in London during June 1980. (Author)

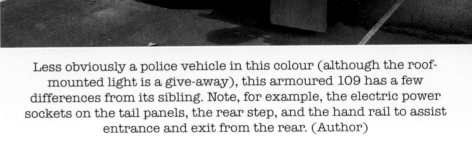

The armoured hardtops were deliberately kitted out with the usual police features of a light bar on the roof and a reflective stripe along each flank. However, from behind it is quite obvious that this is an armoured vehicle, with that heavy door carried on three very substantial hinges. Those slits in the upper body sides are gun ports, and the special deep-dish wheels are an indication of how much extra weight the vehicle is carrying. This vehicle was at one stage lent to the Hampshire Police. (Author)

Less obviously a police vehicle in this colour (although the roof-mounted light is a give-away), this armoured 109 has a few differences from its sibling. Note, for example, the electric power sockets on the tail panels, the rear step, and the hand rail to assist entrance and exit from the rear. (Author)

The Hong Kong Police became the Royal Hong Kong Police in 1969, and continued to take Land Rovers in quantity. The main fleet, of which this Station Wagon is an example, was now painted Navy Blue with a white roof, and the new force crest was displayed on each front door. However, the traffic division's Land Rovers were black with white doors.
(Royal Hong Kong Police)

Based on the Stage 1 V8 109 chassis, this was the RUC's Simba armoured vehicle. There were various minor differences of configuration, and some features altered to meet changing operational requirements.
(Author's collection)

Some examples of the Simba had single rear doors; others had twin doors. This one was photographed after withdrawal from active service. (Author's collection)

own workshops when these were required, and specialist companies were not normally involved.

There were exceptions to this general rule, however. The Provisional Irish Republican Army mounted a sustained terrorist bombing campaign after 1969, both in Northern Ireland and on the British mainland. So the Royal Ulster Constabulary took on a number of armoured Land Rovers, some of which were based on military designs, while others were specially built in its own workshops. Then after the Mogadishu hijacking in 1977, the increased worldwide threat to passenger aircraft from Middle Eastern terrorists persuaded London's Metropolitan Police to buy a small number of armoured Land Rovers. These were, of course, built by a specialist company (Alvis) on the uprated One Ton version of the Series III 109 chassis.

In Northern Ireland, the Royal Ulster Constabulary initially used the appliqué Vehicle Protection Kits designed by the British Army to protect its Series III models. It also bought a small number of Shorland SB301 armoured personnel carriers. These were later supplemented by some Hotspur armoured vehicles on Series III chassis, and then by vehicles of the force's own design, known as the Simba and Shenzi types. Both of these were built on the V8-engined 'Stage 1' 109 chassis in the early 1980s.

Despite the wheelarch eyebrows and the One Ten-type front end, this is actually a very late Series III model. However, it was very special indeed, and probably unique. Built for the Avon & Somerset Police to replace the Series IIA cliff-rescue vehicle pictured in Chapter 2, it had a 126-inch wheelbase, achieved by fitting to a 109 the 17-inch chassis extension that converted a coil-sprung One Ten into a One Two Seven! (Avon & Somerset Police)

Far left: This very early Series III 88 Station Wagon was rigged up to look like an ambulance for publicity pictures, but in fact the only ambulance feature about it was the roof-mounted sign. The 88-inch models were still too small to have much appeal as ambulances. (Jaguar Land Rover)

Left: This Pilcher-Greene design on the 109 chassis had light alloy panels, and was essentially the one that had been introduced in 1964 for military use. This is a left-hand-drive export vehicle. (Pilcher-Greene)

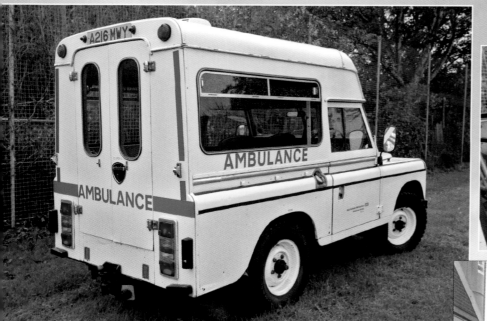

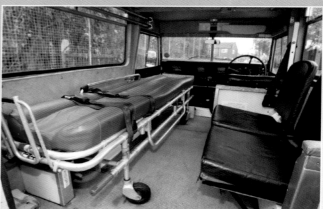

Nevertheless, the West Yorkshire Metropolitan Ambulance Service needed an agile cross-country ambulance for dealing with incidents at remote farmsteads, where narrow gateways were likely to make access difficult – even for a 109-inch Land Rover. So, in 1984, the organisation's own workshops built this very special body on an 88-inch Series III chassis. There was just enough room for a single stretcher after the front passenger seat had been removed, and the attendant had to use an inward-facing seat in the rear on the other side. (Dave Barker/*Land Rover Enthusiast* magazine)

Right: The same basic Pilcher-Greene design did duty as a mobile veterinary clinic, although here it has a roof rack rather than a second-skin 'tropical' roof to minimise the temperature inside the back body. (Pilcher-Greene)

AMBULANCE CONVERSIONS

The demand for cost-effective ambulance conversions remained constant during the 1970s, and the aftermarket specialists evolved new designs that depended on light alloy panels, and were simple to manufacture. By far the majority of Land Rover ambulances were built on the 109-inch chassis, although there were some brave experiments with ambulance bodies on the 88-inch Series III.

Ibis was a new name in the Land Rover ambulance business during the 1970s, and enjoyed success in several overseas countries. This ambulance on a Series III 109 chassis was exported to Portugal, and was pictured in preservation. (José Almeida)

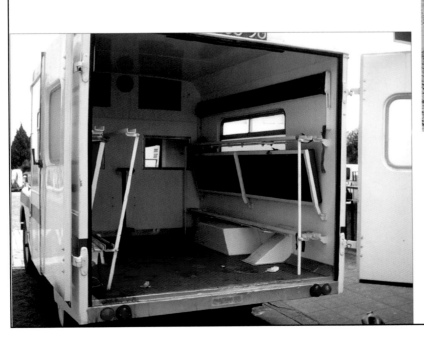

The body on the Ibis ambulances was made of light alloy. The simple but ingenious racking system allowed as many as four stretchers to be carried, and seated patients could be carried instead, or in addition to two stretchers. (Ricardo Teles)

The simple and cost-effective ambulance was still in demand, and this example was built by Herbert Lomas using a Series III 109 window hardtop as a host vehicle. However, it is not quite as simple as it may appear at first sight: the rear of the vehicle has been extended by several inches to give more room in the body, and an air-conditioning system is carried on the cab roof. This left-hand drive example wears sand tyres, and was clearly destined for a Middle Eastern country. (Herbert Lomas Ltd)

Commercial bodybuilder Freight Bonallack also built a batch of ambulances for an overseas order on the 109-inch chassis. These appear to have had light-alloy bodies to a unique design, and also had air-conditioning systems mounted on the roof.
(Freight Bonallack)

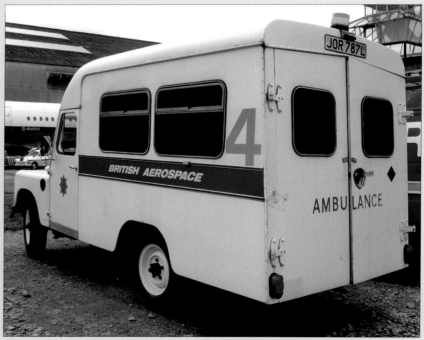

Another new name in the Land Rover ambulance business was Wadham Stringer. The company built this well-proportioned bodywork on a Series III 109 chassis in 1972. It was originally delivered to British Aerospace but has since been transferred to the Brooklands Museum. The front view shows it on site at the War and Peace Show in 2015. (Left: author; right: author's collection)

For rural duties in Spain, a simple Land Rover ambulance fitted the bill perfectly. This 1980 example is a Series III built in Spain by Land Rover's affiliate company, MSA, and sold under the Land Rover Santana brand name. Essentially similar to a UK-built Series III, it nevertheless has detail differences, the moulded GRP roof panel being one of the more obvious. This was a cost-effective two-stretcher design, and a characteristic was white upholstery in the cab. (MSA)

Of the old-established names, both Lomas and Pilchers (now Pilcher-Greene) remained in business. However, the tight hold that the Land Rover approval scheme had held on the business seemed to be relaxing, and some new names appeared. Most important – and with Land Rover Approval – were Wadham Stringer, who were based at Waterlooville in Hampshire.

However, Ibis made some strong inroads into the market, and even non-specialist Freight Bonallack gained a contract to build a batch of ambulances.

As before, the majority of Land Rover ambulances were built for export. However, there was now a new factor at work as well. After 1970, the new Range Rover became available as the basis of a cross-country ambulance, and it added excellent road performance into the equation. Those ambulance authorities which could afford its higher costs therefore tended to favour it over traditional Land Rover-based designs.

The Marshall military ambulance was delivered to the British armed forces in quantity on Series III chassis. There was also a delivery for the Dutch military, of which this is an example. The angled lower rear section was designed to prevent the bodywork catching on the steep loading ramps of aircraft and landing ships. (Marshall)

Chapter 4
THE ONE TEN FAMILY

The first of a new family of Land Rovers was introduced in March 1983 as the Land Rover One Ten. Named after its 110-inch wheelbase, it had a newly-designed chassis that featured coil springs instead of the traditional leaf springs, and permanent four-wheel drive instead of the earlier selectable system. These changes had been brought about by the success of the Range Rover, which featured both.

The One Ten was a replacement for the Series III 109, and it was followed in 1984 by a coil-sprung short-wheelbase Land Rover called the Ninety. Despite its name, the Ninety actually had a 92.9-inch wheelbase; Ninety was of course a more convenient marketing name. There was then a third model on an extended wheelbase of 127 inches from late 1984. Initially known as the One Ten Crew Cab, because it was only available in that configuration, this later became available for other bodywork and was renamed the One Two Seven.

In the early years of the One Ten family, the leaf-sprung Series

III types remained in production as well. However, the Ninety completely replaced the 88-inch in 1984, and the old 109-inch models went out of production during 1985 after existing fleet orders had been met.

Meanwhile, when interest arose in the possibilities of a three-axle Land Rover chassis in the late 1970s, Land Rover's specialist conversions division – known as SVO (Special Vehicle Operations) after July 1985 – kept a close eye on developments. Three-axle chassis, both with undriven third axles and with full six-wheel drive, became available soon after the One Ten was introduced. Land Rover's favoured conversion specialist was Reynolds Boughton, but there were several others. These chassis attracted the attention of fire appliance builders in particular, as they retained the narrow body width and the off-road ability of a standard Land Rover, but also offered a larger carrying capacity for firefighting equipment.

Although no figures are available to confirm this, it seems

probable that there was a major decline in exports of fully-equipped emergency-service Land Rovers during the 1980s. At the start of the decade, changes in UK government aid had radically altered the position in Africa, and Japanese 4x4 manufacturers had moved into that continent quite aggressively in order to offer cheaper options. This caused major problems for Land Rover, which posted its first-ever annual loss in 1983, and although the company was brought back to health by a major re-orientation of its products towards developed countries, its African markets would never be regained.

Back in Britain, the overall picture suggested that customers had begun to avoid the cost of specialist conversions wherever possible. By the end of the 1980s, SVO had also begun to operate a new policy, under which the division would take as much as possible of the Land Rover conversion work (of all kinds) back in-house. This would inevitably have an impact on the work of the conversions specialists as the 1990s opened.

FIRE APPLIANCES

Two trends were noticeable in the Land Rover fire appliance business during the 1980s. The first was that customers were turning towards simpler and less expensive conversions, perhaps reflecting the cost-conscious, value-for-money ethos of the British government of the day. As a result, there were

The short-wheelbase Ninety was not very common in fire service, but this late 1980s example was one of several used by the Marins Pompiers at Marseilles in France. The Marins Pompiers is a unique brigade that is staffed by military personnel from the French Navy. (Chris Warwick)

Pilcher Greene continued to offer its Branbridge designs, slightly modified to suit the 110-inch wheelbase of the Land Rover One Ten. This example dates from the mid-1980s, and was a demonstrator vehicle that carried a Pilcher Greene decal logo below the side locker. (Jaguar Land Rover)

The HCB-Angus designs were no longer branded as Firefly types. This early 1980s example for the fire service in the British Virgin Islands was known simply as a Light Fire Appliance. (HCB-Angus)

fewer major body transformations than in earlier times, and a number of fire appliances were actually created from standard production-line models in the workshops of the user brigades.

The second trend was closely associated with the first, as users began to look at buying three-axle Land Rovers that offered as much space for equipment as traditional larger appliances but were both less expensive and – by virtue of their size – more versatile.

Of the long-standing Land Rover fire appliance specialists, Carmichael, HCB-Angus, and Pilcher Greene all remained in business. These three companies accounted for the majority of specialist fire service conversions on Land Rover chassis during the 1980s.

Carmichael had this simplified design, based on a One Ten hardtop. E76 HLP belonged to the fire and rescue service at the Brooklands Museum in Surrey. (Author)

This One Ten belonged to 1st Defense Fire & Rescue Services, which was based at the Dunsfold Aerodrome in Surrey. It illustrates the 1980s trend towards less complex appliances. The wheels are heavy-duty types of a later specification. (Author)

Again a simple conversion based on a One Ten Station Wagon, this vehicle belonged to the fire service at Alicante in Spain. (Manuel Marcos)

This 1989 One Ten Station Wagon with Diesel Turbo engine belonged to the Royal Berkshire Fire and Rescue Service, and was used among other things for towing the service's breathing apparatus trailer. It was, however, no ordinary Station Wagon, having been specially adapted by Locomotors of Andover. The Godiva fire pump slid out from the rear on a tray when required, and just visible behind it are stowage bins for hoses and other equipment. (Author)

Also belonging to the Royal Berkshire Fire and Rescue Service was this Carmichael appliance based on a V8-engined One Two Seven chassis. The fire pump was mounted at the front of the vehicle presumably to allow better access to equipment carried in the rear. (Author)

The Kent Fire Brigade took a pair of fire appliances based on the One Two Seven chassis, each with a Quadtec back body built by Land Rover's own Special Vehicle Operations division. The Quadtec was a versatile 'box' that could be made in different sizes to meet different uses. (Jaguar Land Rover)

Despite the trend towards simplicity, it was during the 1980s that the six-wheel Land Rover fire appliances began to attract customers. The basis of this one was a 6x6 chassis conversion by Reynolds Boughton, who also built the body. It provided fire cover at the Longbridge factory then owned by the Rover Group. (Reynolds Boughton)

F98 DKN was one of the two Quadtec-bodied One Two Sevens delivered to the Kent Fire Brigade. It was pictured after acquisition by 1st Defense Fire & Rescue Services at Dunsfold. The simple Quadtec design was produced to meet the trend towards less expensive conversions. (Author)

This six-wheeler spent some time as a Land Rover demonstrator. It was a joint product of Land Rover's own Special Vehicle Operations and HCB-Angus, although the six-wheel chassis was probably built by Reynolds Boughton under sub-contract.
(Jaguar Land Rover)

The Dorset Fire Brigade took a pair of six-wheel fire tenders with bodywork by HCB-Angus. F338 VFX was pictured in one of is annual haunts – the fairground at the Great Dorset Steam Fair.
(Author)

Not every fire tender has to be red ... This one is on the special One Ten 6x6 chassis created in Australia, initially to meet a military requirement. It belonged to the National Parks and Wildlife Service and would have been used for fighting bush fires. It was affectionately named Lofty by its crew.
(Land Rover Australia)

The sheer size of the Australian 6x6 chassis allowed a large amount of firefighting equipment to be carried. This demonstrator vehicle had a noticeably wide rear body.
(Land Rover Australia)

POLICE VEHICLES

British police forces remained big Land Rover customers during the 1980s, but the majority of their purchases were of Range Rovers. The Ninety gained a following as a useful vehicle for rural policing, while the One Ten remained of interest when extra carrying capacity was needed, or the vehicle had to be armoured, as in Northern Ireland. Police forces also began to take an interest in the new One Two Seven with its ultra-long-wheelbase, because this offered additional load capacity for specialist uses.

The Ninety quickly earned orders from UK police forces, especially once it became available with the 3.5-litre V8 engine. This gave it a decent turn of speed and also low-down pulling power for towing. This Metropolitan Police Station Wagon dates from 1986, and has the characteristic rubber push-bars of that force's traffic division vehicles. (Metropolitan Police)

By contrast, a four-cylinder engine provided all the performance needed for rural policing duties. This Ninety hardtop was used for exactly that by the Northamptonshire Police. (Jaguar Land Rover)

The South Yorkshire Police also took Ninetys for rural policing duties. This one has the Station Wagon configuration. (Roger Conway)

Most unusual was this 1987 Ninety, used by the Merseyside Police. The roof platform and ladders would have been used by SWAT teams to gain access to the upper floors of a building. It probably did not get a lot of use, which explains why a redundant front spoiler from a car has been dumped beneath it. (PVEC/Alex McKenzie)

Clark Masts offered an overhead illumination system that could be attached to a One Ten. In this case, the vehicle is a demonstrator and probably not a real police Land Rover. The mast was elevated hydraulically. (Clark Masts Teksam)

The long-wheelbase Land Rover remained the police favourite, and this early One Ten Station Wagon belonged to the Thames Valley Police. It has a Dale Stemlite mounted on the roof – a floodlight system mounted on an extending pole that could be used to illuminate an accident scene at night. (Thames Valley Police)

The long-wheelbase hardtop still remained a useful police vehicle, and this example was bought by the West Midlands Police. Interesting features are the front-mounted self-recovery winch, and the military-pattern side locker ahead of the rear wheel. (PVEC)

Even though the Range Rover had taken over as the primary motorway patrol vehicle, Cumbria Constabulary could still see a need for One Ten Station Wagons. This 1986 example watches over a stretch of M6 motorway as darkness falls. (Jaguar Land Rover)

A quite different configuration features on this One Ten for the Royal Oman Police. The vehicle is a pick-up with a substantial rollover bar behind the cab. (Jaguar Land Rover)

The requirement for armoured patrol vehicles remained constant in Northern Ireland, and the RUC used the One Ten as the basis of its Tangi vehicle. This one was pictured on operational duty in the province, with another armoured RUC type in the background. (Author's collection)

In early 2000, the Police Service of Northern Ireland (PSNI), which had succeeded the RUC, repainted the Tangi fleet in more generic police colours that incorporated 'Battenburg' reflective side panels. This example shows the result. It had been used in a demonstration of fire-resistant materials, and the burning at the front end shows typical damage from a petrol bomb of the type sometimes used during riots. (Author's collection)

The terrorist threat changed during the 1980s but did not recede, and most police forces took on at least one armoured Land Rover. This One Ten belonged to the Thames Valley Police, and is seen here parked with the usual block against the rear wheel. These vehicles were so heavy that it was unwise to trust the handbrake on its own! (PVEC/Roger Young)

Many of the Tangi vehicles were sold off for re-use, as stability returned to Northern Ireland. These two were taken on by the West Yorkshire Police and were re-registered on the UK mainland. (PVEC/Steve Pearson)

Land Rover SVO's Quadtec body was here used to good effect on the One Two Seven chassis to create a mobile command post for the Devon & Cornwall Police. The vehicle was new in 1986. (Jaguar Land Rover)

The 127-inch Land Rover also had its police uses. This 1985 model was, strictly, a One Ten Crew Cab, and was fitted with a hardtop over its standard pick-up back body. It belonged to the Mersey Tunnel Police, but had almost certainly started life as a Land Rover demonstrator. (Mersey Tunnel Police)

AMBULANCE CONVERSIONS

The desire to drive down costs was particularly apparent in the ambulance business. To meet this, SVO came up with a cost-effective in-house conversion based on a One Ten Station Wagon, while MMB International developed a high-roof One Ten Station Wagon conversion that could be adapted for multiple uses besides that of an ambulance.

The need for lower costs also persuaded Wadham Stringer of Waterlooville in Hampshire to develop a 4x4 ambulance that would be less expensive than those it was already building on Range Rover chassis. Its choice fell on the new Land Rover One Two Seven chassis. Of the long-standing converters, Pilcher Greene remained the most prolific builder of ambulances on the One Ten chassis. The company had a range of options, from a simple tall hardtop on a pick-up, to a fully coachbuilt ambulance – although by this stage 'coachbuilt' meant extensive use of GRP and light alloy outer panels over a steel frame.

Herbert Lomas announced an ambulance conversion on the One Ten but probably did not make very many of them, as this long-established company was wound up in about

1983. From the ashes of this company (originally at Handforth but latterly at Congleton) MMB (Macclesfield Motor Bodies) was formed. Trading as MMB International, this company developed a modular ambulance design to suit both the One Ten and One Two Seven chassis, and which went on to gain Land Rover approval, and to sell well.

The One Two Seven chassis also attracted interest from military authorities around the world, that needed its additional space to create ambulances. As a result, several new designs became available.

Special Vehicle Operations converted this One Ten Station Wagon into an ambulance, but, livery and light bar apart, there were no obvious external signs. Only the dark 'privacy' glass seems to be not part of the standard Station Wagon specification. This one probably did time as a Land Rover demonstrator before going to the St John Ambulance division at Ambleside. (Roger Conway)

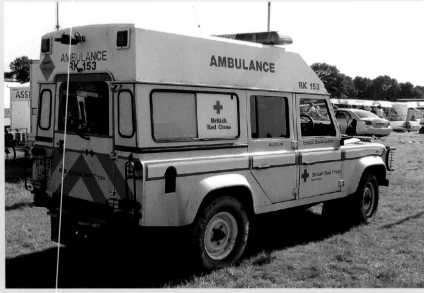

Simplicity and cost-effectiveness remained the rules of the game in the 1980s. This GRP roof extension was by MMB and minimised the amount of work needed to turn a Station Wagon into a credible ambulance with standing room. G468 UKE belonged to the Kent Branch of the British Red Cross, and was pictured on two separate occasions, wearing different call-sign identification above the front door. (Author)

Not every vehicle used by an ambulance service was actually an ambulance. The Derbyshire Ambulance Service used this early One Ten hardtop to tow its Incident Control unit.
(Alastair Green)

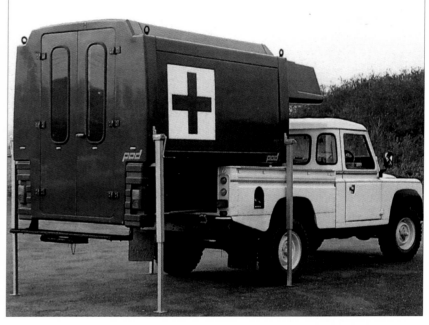

Another cost-effective idea of the period was this demountable ambulance pod, made by Shanning. The host vehicle is a One Ten High-Capacity Pick-Up, and the pod is finished in green to appeal to military customers. Civilian versions were of course available as well. (Shanning Pod)

This is a 1990-model One Ten Station Wagon, with the '110' bonnet badge used only that year. Such vehicles were ideal for the St John Ambulance Brigade, which here was providing cover at a summer classic transport rally.
(Author)

The simplest of the Pilcher Greene ambulance conversions was once again a hardtop that could be added to a standard pick-up body. It was known as the Type 8404B or, more simply, the B-type body. This one is mounted on an early left-hand-drive One Ten, and has the tropical roof panels on cab and back body that were normally supplied to hot countries.
(Pilcher Greene)

Next up in the cost hierarchy from Pilcher Greene was the 8404F or F-type body, moulded from GRP. The sliding door windows once again reveal this one to be mounted on an early One Ten. (Pilcher Greene)

The most expensive of the Pilcher Greene options was this one, which was known as the 8303S or S-type. It had a welded steel body frame on which were mounted GRP and aluminium alloy outer panels, while the interior lining was in plastic laminate. (Pilcher Greene)

MMB International developed a range of modular ambulance bodies for the Land Rover range, distinguished by their angular cab roof design. This the C-type body on a One Ten chassis, with light alloy exterior panels. Various different interior configurations were available, and this example has an air-conditioning unit mounted on the roof. (MMB International)

Maximum flexibility reduced manufacturing costs, and the MMB C-type ambulance was also available for military users. The major difference was an absence of side widows in the ambulance body, and there is no illuminated Ambulance sign above the cab, either. (MMB International)

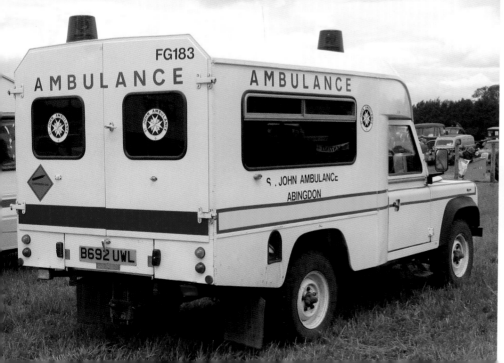

This 1985 Pilcher Greene-bodied One Ten was used by the Abingdon division of the St John Ambulance Brigade to provide cover at outdoor events over the summer. (Author)

This Pilcher Greene 8303S ambulance has a Hubbard CU170 air-conditioning unit mounted on the roof, as commonly specified for hot countries. It was destined for Ras al Khaimah in the United Arab Emirates. (Pilcher Greene)

Lomas also built a few ambulances on the One Ten chassis, and this one had a particularly neat design. Note how the body was extended by several inches at the rear to improve internal space. (Herbert Lomas)

When Land Rover introduced its extended-wheelbase One Two Seven chassis in 1984, Wadham Stringer saw the opportunity to create a more spacious ambulance at far less cost than its extended-wheelbase Range Rover conversion. This one was an early example that was taken on by the Suffolk Ambulance Service. (Wadham Stringer)

Dating from later in the 1980s, and with a different blue-light system on the roof, this Wadham Stringer One Two Seven belonged to the St John Ambulance division at Stratford-on-Avon. The deep sill panel below the door was a characteristic of this conversion. (Michael Jaye)

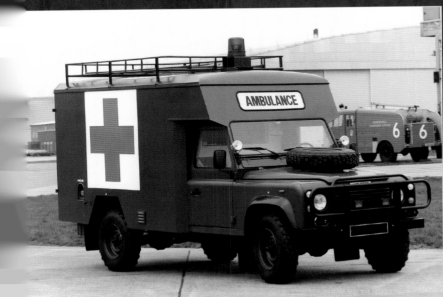

The British armed forces took a quantity of 127 ambulances with bodies built by Marshall of Cambridge. Later deliveries had a broadly similar (but not identical) body by Locomotors of Andover. This is a Marshall body. (Nick Dimbleby)

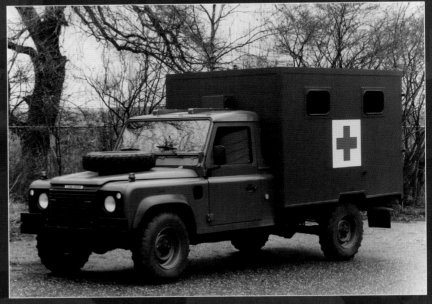

Marshall also supplied the ambulance bodies for a Dutch military order, but they had a very different design to the British ones. The base vehicle was again a 127. (Marshall)

Chapter 5
DEFENDER

The Defender range was an improved continuation of the One Ten family of the 1980s. Introduced in 1990, it was characterised in the beginning by having a 2.5-litre '200Tdi' direct-injection diesel engine as standard. The Defender name was chosen to harmonise with that of the new mid-range Land Rover, the Discovery, and reflected the utility models' regular use by defence forces around the world.

What had earlier been called Ninety, One Ten and One Two Seven now became Defender 90, Defender 110 and Defender 130. There was no increase in the wheelbase for the largest of these; it was simply that the figure was rounded up for marketing purposes. Defenders also had relocated cab seating to give more elbow-room, and they carried the latest version of the Land Rover green oval badge on the grille and tail panel.

The 200Tdi engine was replaced during 1994 by the more refined, but no more powerful, 300Tdi type, and this in turn gave way to the five-cylinder Td5 in 1998. Again, this had a 2.5-litre capacity. For the 2007 models, the engine became the Ford-built TDCi or Puma diesel, which was taller than the earlier engines, and was covered by a new bonnet incorporating a bulge. This engine then gave way to a similarly powered 2.2-litre TDCi in 2012, which met tighter new exhaust emission regulations.

For much of the 1990s, the Defender could be had to special order with the old 3.5-litre carburettor version of the V8 engine. Stocks of this eventually ran out, and the four-cylinder turbocharged diesel became the only option. Defender production was brought to an end in January 2016.

From the start of Defender production, it was Land Rover policy to take more and more of the conversion work in-house. As a result, specialist conversions became Special Vehicle Operations (SVO) conversions; with reorganisation at Land Rover, the controlling body became Land Rover Special Vehicles (LRSV) from 1992. Several of the earlier conversion specialists continued to work on Land Rovers, but they had to do so as junior partners to LRSV, and as sub-contractors.

The Northumberland Fire and Rescue Service used this 1991 Defender 90 hardtop as a support vehicle. The checker plate on bonnet and front wings provided strength in case firefighters needed to stand on the vehicle. (Roger Conway)

FIRE APPLIANCES

The decline continued in the number of conversions based on the two smaller sizes of Land Rover – the Defender 90 and Defender 110. Although some examples were taken on by fire services, they tended to be used for administrative or towing duties, and few were converted into actual firefighting appliances. Nevertheless, reflecting the success of the Land Rover company's turnaround after its early 1980s difficulties, exports of Defender-based fire appliances increased, most notably to continental Europe.

The most popular version of the Defender with fire services was the largest, the 130, but even in this case there were relatively few specially converted vehicles. In most cases, the Defender 130s taken on by fire services were standard production vehicles, that were adapted as simply as possible.

For those who needed a larger appliance, six-wheel chassis were still available, and long-serving converters such as Carmichael would build special bodywork for them – although the Carmichael company did not survive in its original form beyond 2004. Defender six-wheel fire tenders were taken on

This Defender 90 Station Wagon belonged to the Vigili del Fuoco, the Italian national fire and rescue service. It was nevertheless not equipped as a fire appliance, but was used primarily for administrative duties. (Author's collection)

to provide fire cover on factory sites, and notably at several of Britain's car factories. Land Rover Special Vehicles coordinated the build of these vehicles as far as it was able, but several were built by GB Fire on chassis converted to three-axle configuration by Penman Engineering.

Again with no visible signs of firefighting equipment, this Defender 110 belonged to the fire service at Faro in Portugal. It is a Td5-engined model dating from between 1998 and 2006. (Des Penny)

Carmichael continued to provide a basic fire tender conversion of the Defender 110, based on the standard pick-up model. (Carmichael)

In the Defender era, the extended-wheelbase Defender 130 became the favourite as the basis of fire appliances. This example belonged to the volunteer fire service at Figueira da Foz in Portugal, and was a straightforward conversion of the 130 pick-up. (Author's collection)

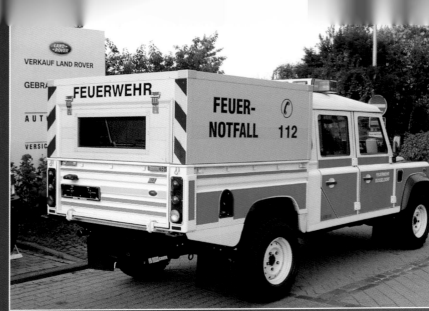

Dating from 2005, this Defender 130 was pictured before delivery to the fire service in Düsseldorf, Germany. The conversion of a standard crew cab model with pick-up rear body was confined to the addition of a box-like hardtop to protect equipment carried in the rear. (Stefan Schumacher)

Staffordshire Fire and Rescue bought a small quantity of these appliances in 2003. Based on the Defender 130 with Td5 engine, they were designed and built by Land Rover Special Vehicles. A notable feature is the sturdy external rollover cage. (Jaguar Land Rover)

This 2009 Defender 130 belonged to the Hereford & Worcester Fire and Rescue Service, and had the 2.4-litre Puma or TDCi diesel engine. It was an essentially standard production vehicle, with a demountable pod in the rear containing all the firefighting equipment. (Author)

Once again belonging to the Italian Vigili del Fuoco, this is a Defender 130 crew cab. It was probably used for towing the boat seen in the background of the picture. (Jaguar Land Rover)

Towing a boat was typical of the duties assigned to this Defender 130 crew cab belonging to the French fire service at Perpignan. (Jochen von Arnim)

Carmichael built this rather attractive Defender 130 for the fire service at the St Fergus offshore gas terminal in Aberdeenshire. (Carmichael)

This Australian-built 130 has a 'big cab' that was built locally. The back body carries special equipment for dealing with chemical incidents and others involving hazardous materials. (Land Rover Australia)

This Defender 130-based appliance is fairly typical of those prepared in Australia for rural fire brigades. The open back body gives rapid access to equipment used in fighting bush fires. (Patrick Sutcliffe)

Left: The six-wheel Land Rover remained popular during the Defender era. This example was a Carmichael confection for the fire brigade at Harare in Zimbabwe. (Carmichael)

Below: Built in 2000, this six-wheel tender provided fire cover at BMW's Hams Hall engine plant. It was built by GB Fire on a chassis converted by Penman Engineering. (John Carter)

Above and right: This rather earlier example built by GB Fire on a six-wheel Defender chassis provided fire cover at Land Rover's own Solihull factory. The left-side picture shows it on duty at the factory, with side lockers open to display its equipment. By the time of the right-side picture, it had been fitted with the later design of heavy-duty wheels. (Above: John Carter; right: Jaguar Land Rover)

POLICE VEHICLES

Demand from police forces for Defenders held up quite well during the 1990s, although several customers began to investigate other, less expensive, options. When the British Army began to sell off examples of its 'Snatch' armoured vehicles – originally designed for use in Northern Ireland but under-protected for duties in Afghanistan and Iran – a number were snapped up by UK police forces. This was to meet a Home Office guideline that each force should have at least one armoured vehicle on its fleet.

The right vehicle for the job ... this Thames Valley Police Defender 90 Station Wagon was pictured on duty in July 1997 at the Bloxham Steam Rally. The churned-up mud makes clear why the Defender was so useful for rural police work. (Author)

Showing yet another variation of light bar and livery, this Defender 90 Station Wagon from the mid-1990s belonged to the Durham Constabulary. (Roger Conway)

This later Defender 90 belonging to the Lancashire Constabulary was one of the first to have the Td5 five-cylinder engine. In this case, the force favoured a hardtop model. The vehicle is essentially standard apart from the additional lights and a police radio. (Roger Conway)

Land Rover was particularly pleased to get a contract to supply Defender 90 Station Wagons to the Carabinieri in Italy. The Carabinieri was used to petrol engines, and so all the first batch were specially fitted with the 2-litre T16 four-cylinder Rover Cars engine, although later examples were Tdi diesel powered. (Author's collection)

The Defender 90 earned an order from the Portuguese Police, and the example pictured here shows the bonnet marking to advantage. It was readily recognisable from the air, and also served to warn drivers who looked in the mirror that there was a police vehicle behind them. (Norman Hinchcliffe)

The French Gendarmerie took a number of Defenders in the mid-1990s; this 110 and 90 were pictured at a dealer's premises before delivery via Rover France. (Jaguar Land Rover)

Now with full Gendarmerie markings, this is the same Defender 110 as that on the left. It was used for mountain rescue work. (Jaguar Land Rover)

Another mid-1990s Defender 110 Station Wagon in police service, this time owned by the Surrey Constabulary. (Author)

A Defender helps out at an open-air event again. This Defender 110 belonged to the Dorset Police, and was pictured on duty during the annual Great Dorset Steam Fair. The markings on its rear panels show that its main purpose was recovery of stranded vehicles on the site. (Author)

This Defender 110 Station Wagon was part of a sizeable order for the Angolan Police delivered in 1996. The wire mesh over the rear side windows and headlamps suggests that it was intended for use in areas where violence was expected. **Below:** The two Defender 110s were from the same Angolan order. Both are 110 pick-ups with truck cabs, one with a windowed tilt in place. Once again, there is protective mesh over the headlamps. (Author)

This time featuring the 'Battenburg' reflective marking scheme, this 2003 Td5-engined Defender 110 belonged to the Thames Valley Police. It was pictured at another outdoor summer show in Oxfordshire. (Author)

Courtaulds provided the light armour on V8-engined Defender 110s for the British Army. These were known familiarly as 'Snatch' vehicles because of their use in 'snatching' trouble-makers from the streets in Northern Ireland. When they were sold off, several went to mainland police forces, and this 1994 example went to the Kent Police. (Author)

This formidable-looking armoured Defender 110 belonged to the Greater Manchester Police, and was fully equipped for use by an armed response unit. (PVEC)

The requirement for armoured police Land Rovers did not go away, and this example was new in around 2008 to the Hampshire Police. (PVEC/Brian Homans)

The Pangolin armoured personnel carrier was developed by Ovik in Dorset, initially for use with the PSNI, who took a large quantity from 2011. This batch of three, all registered by the makers, was new in 2012 to the Merseyside Police. The chassis is an uprated Defender 110, and the engine a 2.4-litre TDCi diesel. (PVEC)

AMBULANCE CONVERSIONS

The major ambulance conversions on Defender chassis were for military users, and they included both custom-built and demountable-body types. In the civilian market, the most prolific British supplier was MMB International, which had a range of cleverly-designed modular bodies for the Defender 110 and Defender 130 chassis. As Land Rover's penetration of continental European markets deepened, so some ambulance specialists in those countries also created bodies for the Defender.

Top left: In 2008, Land Rover marked its 60th anniversary as a brand by donating 60 ambulances to the International Federation of Red Cross and Red Crescent Societies. A small number, like this one, remained in Britain. It is a Defender 110 Station Wagon with the 2.4-litre TDCi diesel engine. (Author)

Top right: Yet another Defender 110 Station Wagon, this one belonging to the British Red Cross. The picture again makes the point of the Land Rover's value to emergency services when the going gets tough.
(Jaguar Land Rover)

Left: The shot is posed, of course, but it does illustrate the value of a Defender ambulance in reaching the scene of an incident in difficult terrain. Once again, the vehicle is a 110 Station Wagon, although the conversion by SVO allows it to carry a stretcher trolley in the back. (Jaguar Land Rover)

Defender 110 Station Wagons with various degrees of internal conversion were widely used by both volunteer and full-time rescue services. This one was in use for that purpose in Australia. (ULR, Melbourne)

Not every ambulance had to be white ... this one provided medical cover on a beach in the Gard region of southern France. The local fire brigade had responsibility for rescue operations, and the signwriting explains that this Defender 110 window hardtop provided emergency aid to those who had been injured or had been rescued from drowning. (Le Commandant Martin, Sapeurs Pompiers du Gard)

MMB International continued to supply its GRP roof to improve the headroom in Defender 110 ambulance conversions. This one was probably a Land Rover SVO demonstrator. (Larry Court)

The MMB C type body remained available for the Defender, and is seen here on a Defender 130 chassis. However, the implication of cooperating with Land Rover's newly re-organised SVO division was that the division took the credit for vehicles produced under sub-contract. The signwriting on the sill describes this as 'A Conversion by Land Rover Special Vehicle Operations.' (Jaguar Land Rover)

The Defender's value as an ambulance was widely appreciated overseas, too. This French-registered example was bodied by Sanicar, a division of the Gruau group. (Author's collection)

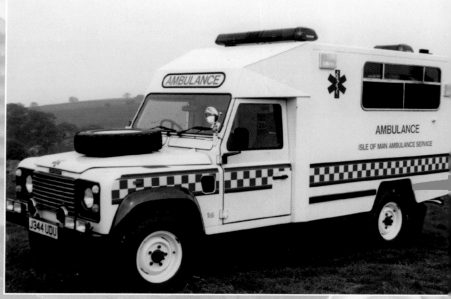

This is another variation of the MMB type C body on Defender 130 chassis, in this case without the equipment locker access immediately behind the cab. (MMB International)

This view of the interior of an MMB C type body on the Defender 130 shows how the space was utilised to maximum effect. (Author)

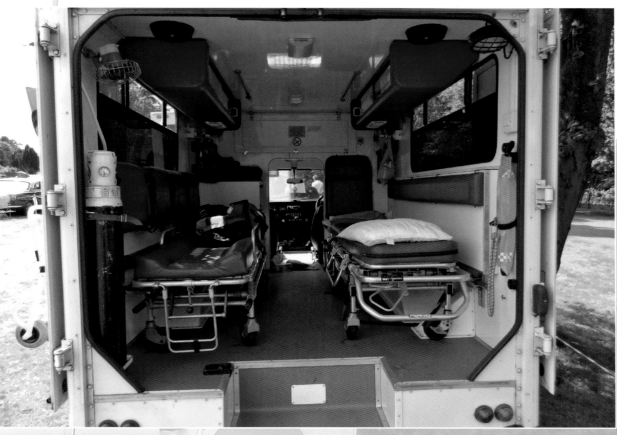

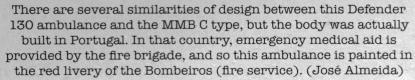

There are several similarities of design between this Defender 130 ambulance and the MMB C type, but the body was actually built in Portugal. In that country, emergency medical aid is provided by the fire brigade, and so this ambulance is painted in the red livery of the Bombeiros (fire service). (José Almeida)

By the time this Defender 130 ambulance was built, the Td5 diesel engine was the standard fitment. Once again, the body was built in Portugal, this time for the ambulance service at Gouveia. (José Almeida)

Pictured at a display of Land Rover conversions, this Defender 130 has a demountable ambulance body – another idea for reducing costs. (Jaguar Land Rover)

When the British Army needed a new Battlefield Ambulance in the mid-1990s, this Defender 130 with body by Marshall of Cambridge won the contract. It was developed under the code name of Pulse, and was based on the Defender XD (heavy-duty) chassis. The crosses that identify it as an ambulance are concealed under their hinged panels (just behind the window in the body) in this picture. (Roger Conway)

Inset: The Pulse military ambulance had a versatile interior, with accommodation for up to four stretchers. (Jaguar Land Rover)

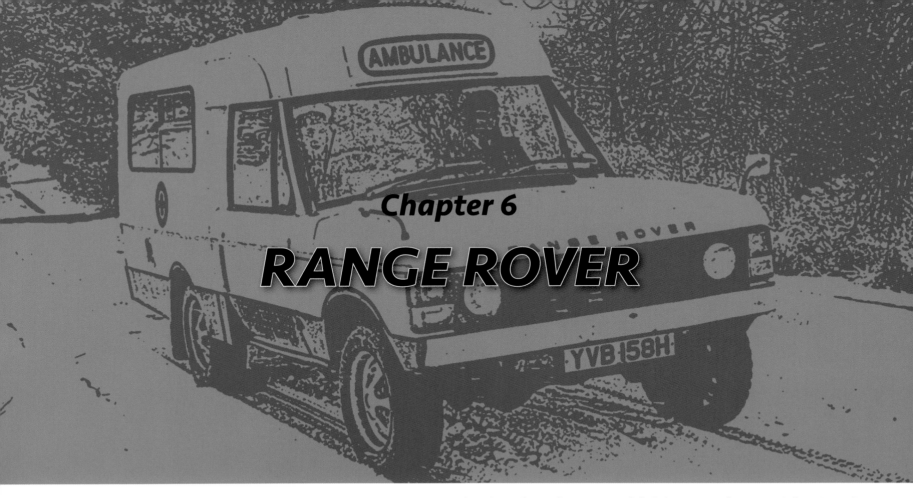

Chapter 6
RANGE ROVER

The Range Rover was developed as a more comfortable Land Rover station wagon, with better road performance, and was introduced in June 1970. Its basic design was a five-seat station wagon or estate car. Improved ride comfort came from long-travel coil-spring suspension, and strong road performance came from the 3.5-litre V8 petrol engine that the Rover Company had bought from General Motors' Buick division in the mid-1960s. Meanwhile, a permanent four-wheel-drive system allowed the use of lighter-duty axles, which in turn improved ride quality. The vehicle had disc brakes all round, and a self-energising ride-levelling system on the rear axle.

All early Range Rovers had just two doors, despite their four/five-seat configuration. Customer demand led Land Rover to develop a four-door model that was introduced in 1981, which quickly became the best-seller, and the two-door was relegated to export and special-purpose duties until it was withdrawn in 1994. After Land Rover's reorientation towards developed markets in the mid-1980s, the Range Rover was relentlessly

developed as a luxury model. Prices rose, but special stripped-out versions remained available for emergency-service users and others. However, by 1990 Land Rover had stopped providing the chassis-cabs on which fire and ambulance conversions had been based, although the Range Rover remained available with a special police specification.

The engine was a 3.5-litre V8, with around 130bhp between 1970 and 1988 (the power figure varied over time). However, from 1985 a 165bhp injected version became available on top models, and from 1989 this gave way to a 180bhp injected 3.9-litre type. There was also a 4.2-litre size, with 200bhp from 1992, but this was normally confined to the special long-wheelbase (Vogue LSE) limousine models. A diesel option became available in 1986; initially this was a 112bhp 2.4-litre, which was then enlarged to a 2.5-litre with 119bhp in 1989. From 1992 a different 2.5-litre diesel with 111bhp was introduced.

Most Range Rovers had steel coil springs, but top models,

including the Vogue LSE, had electronically-controlled air suspension from 1992. The last examples were built in early 1996, by which time the original model had already been superseded by a second-generation version, that had far less appeal to the emergency services.

FIRE APPLIANCES

In the beginning, Land Rover tried to develop the Range Rover in much the same way as it had with the Land Rover, treating it as an adaptable platform suitable for conversions. It became clear early on that the vehicle was too small to make a satisfactory fire appliance, but specialists Carmichael worked with Land Rover to create a three-axle chassis that provided the necessary body space. This was developed as both a fire tender and, more notably, as a Rapid Intervention Vehicle (RIV) for use at airfields and airports. The Carmichael chassis was known as the Commando type.

Carmichael normally provided the bodywork for the fire tenders and RIV vehicles, although under a contract with the British Ministry of Defence, a large number of examples were bodied by Gloster Saro and HCB-Angus. These vehicles were used by all three branches of the armed services, and were known as TACR-2 (carburettor engine) and TACR-2A (injected engine) types. The letters stood for Truck, Airfield Crash Rescue.

Even the production design of Commando RIV evolved. This 1978 version, also used at Cambridge Airport, lacks the windows at the rear of the cab, and doesn't have the roof monitor or the front extension carrying a fire pump. (Richard Webber)

The prototype Carmichael Commando was converted from a pilot-production Range Rover, YVB 152H. It originally had a hand-made alloy body, but this was written-off in an accident, and the vehicle was rebodied with the 'production' style of GRP bodywork. In its later years, it served at Cambridge Airport. (Richard Webber)

The side lockers were generously sized on the standard Commando RIV. This is one on the 1978 model at Cambridge Airport. (Richard Webber)

31AG 60 is a TACR-2 that served with the RAF. In this picture, the distinctive Niphan connector of these vehicles can be seen as a red box at the rear. It allowed systems to be kept warm electrically so that the vehicle was always ready for service, and the connection would pull out automatically and safely if the vehicle was driven off without first being unplugged! (Author)

Different, yet again, is this example used by BAC at its Filton Aerodrome. It has both roof monitor and front-mounted pump, and has twin lockers on each side instead of a single one. (BAC)

Not every Carmichael Commando actually carried the appropriate badging, but this badge was pictured on one that did. It was fitted in place of the plate badge on each side of the scuttle, seen on Range Rovers up to mid-1979. (Author)

LDF 681P was the first of a dozen six-wheel Range Rovers built by Gloster Saro to a near-military specification, but which were actually delivered to British Aerospace airfields. Originally at the BAe (Hawker Siddeley) Dunsfold aerodrome, it was donated to the Brooklands Museum Fire Service in 1995. Like the early TACR-2s, it has a four-door cab but is based on a two-door body. (Matt Emmerson)

Dating from 1988, this Commando was delivered to the Falkland Islands. It has the later body configuration, based on a four-door Range Rover. The vehicle was latterly used mainly as a road-accident response tender, and is now in preservation in the UK: in this picture, it is wearing its original Falklands registration plate as well as its UK number. (Jaguar Land Rover)

POLICE VEHICLES

Land Rover recognised the potential of the Range Rover as a police vehicle early on, and began to solicit interest from Britain's police forces as early as 1968, some two years before the model entered production. It created quite a stir in police circles, and the writer of an early report in *Police Review* claimed that, "In all the years I have been road-testing vehicles I have never come across such a universally-acceptable, or ready-made, police vehicle as the Range Rover."

The Range Rover rapidly became a favourite as a motorway patrol car, combining a good turn of speed with the ability to carry emergency equipment, and also the ability to tow (or push) heavy vehicles off the carriageway when necessary. Sales were good in some European countries as well as in Britain, and Land Rover was anxious not to lose these as the Range Rover moved further upmarket, and became more expensive. So there was a special police-specification Range Rover right through to the end of production, stripped of most of the luxury features, and latterly equipped with the diesel engine option.

Two special rescue tenders were built on Commando chassis for the Swiss railways authority. They were used for emergency duties in the mountains and, particularly, to gain access to the long railway tunnels in those mountains. The bodies were built by Hess of Solothurn. (Author)

The West Mercia Constabulary took Range Rovers from 1971, and this 1974 example is in the force's distinctive and unusual orange and white livery. West Mercia vehicles later played a major role in the Central Motorway Patrol Group. (PVEC/Bob Chambers)

Some police Range Rovers were used for special purposes. Greater Manchester Police, for example, had a two-door van version that was used by its armed support unit, while the Kent County Constabulary bought no fewer than four Vogue LSE (long-wheelbase) models that were designated as Incident Command Vehicles, and may have been the only LSE models in police service.

Police motorway patrol Range Rovers carried a vast amount of equipment for dealing with incidents on the motorway. When not in use, it was stowed in the load bay, in racks made to suit by the force's own workshops. This West Mercia vehicle shows both racks and equipment. (PVEC/Paul Yarrington)

The vehicle in this picture belonged to the Metropolitan Police, and the equipment is slightly different, in this case including a pair of floodlights. A stiff broom was always carried, for clearing debris from the carriageway after an accident. (PVEC)

C425 UKV was originally a Land Rover demonstrator, but was eventually purchased by the Cumbria Police, and is seen here on duty on a foggy M6 motorway near Shap. (JLR)

Range Rovers were also used by the Belgian Gendarmerie. Most had a Dale Stem-Lite on the roof like this one; it raised floodlights on a hydraulic mast to illuminate the area around the vehicle when the crew was dealing with an incident at night. (Luc Geraerts)

The Dutch Rijkspolitie (State Police) used Range Rovers, too. This example was preserved in the force's museum collection. (Maarten van Hoogen)

The Dale Stem-Lite is seen in extended mode here on a two-door Range Rover belonging to the Humberside Police. The 'Stem' part of the name stood for Storable Telescopic Extending Mast. (JLR)

Yet another livery is seen on this Cheshire Police motorway patrol Range Rover. It is a 1993 four-door model, with the 200Tdi diesel engine and the Discovery-style steel wheels that were standard on late police-specification diesel models. (Jaguar Land Rover)

The Lancashire Constabulary was a long-term user of Range Rovers for motorway patrol work. Its last one, N901 FFR, was delivered in November 1995. (Roger Conway)

The Ministry of Defence Police had a number of armoured Range Rovers for escort duties, which primarily involved escorting nuclear materials as they were transported around the country. This 1985 example was based on the 110-inch wheelbase ambulance chassis, and was armoured by MacNeillie's of Walsall. (PVEC/Eric McIntosh)

AMBULANCE CONVERSIONS

Just as it had found when developing fire-service conversions of the Range Rover, Land Rover quickly discovered that the Range Rover was too small to make a viable ambulance. However, the company considered that there was good potential in the ambulance market, and for that reason developed an extended-chassis model with a 110-inch wheelbase.

This provided the necessary length in the body (although it was often accompanied by an extended rear overhang as well), and several ambulance specialists did well with it. Wadham Stringer, Herbert Lomas and Pilcher Greene all developed

designs. The Special Projects department also came up with its own multi-purpose body that could be used as an ambulance, but remained rare. Ibis, meanwhile, developed a design on the standard wheelbase that had a very long rear overhang, and probably for that reason was not awarded Land Rover approval.

There was demand for even bigger ambulances from Scandinavia and continental Europe, and Heinel in Sweden developed its own 139-inch wheelbase chassis to suit the body its customers wanted. Back in Britain, Land Rover developed a 135-inch wheelbase chassis, and this was bodied by Wadham Stringer and Herbert Lomas, as well as by Emil Frey in Switzerland.

The prototype 110-inch ambulance was converted from a pre-production Range Rover and was bodied by Wadham Stringer. It served for a time at the Rover factory, and later belonged to the Worcester City branch of the British Red Cross. The conditions here show why such vehicles were sometimes necessary, even in Britain. (Dave Shephard)

Land Rover also drew up a versatile GRP body that could be used as a shooting brake or, as here, an ambulance. Built by Spencer Abbott, FXC 831L became the factory demonstrator, but attracted no orders. It later served with the St John's Ambulance brigade at Stratford-on Avon. (Author)

Access to the rear of the Spencer Abbott ambulance was by means of a hinged top tailgate and short bottom tailgate. (Author)

Pilcher Greene became a key player in the Range Rover ambulance market. This was its CS type body, made from GRP. (Pilcher Greene)

Herbert Lomas was also quick off the mark with an ambulance body for the Range Rover. This was an early example, possibly the first. (Author's collection)

The Lomas body could carry a single gurney plus three seated patients, which was fairly typical for Range Rover ambulances on the 110-inch wheelbase. Access was through a large hinged rear door. (Author's collection)

This later Herbert Lomas ambulance was exported to Dubai. The body design had not changed: note the characteristic fluting just behind the door top. (Jaguar Land Rover)

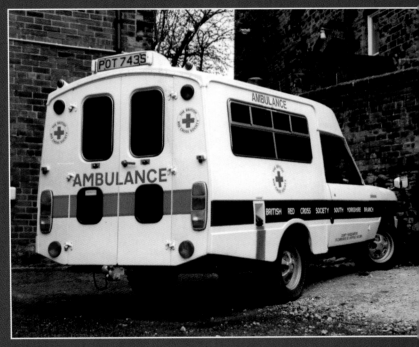

This early 1980s Wadham Stringer ambulance belonged to the Derbyshire Ambulance Service, where it would have been used particularly in the remoter parts of the Peak District. The square leading edge to the body behind the door is a distinguishing characteristic of the Wadham Stringer design. (Alastair Green)

The Wadham Stringer rear end design was quite different from the Lomas type, and featured twin rear doors. (Author's collection)

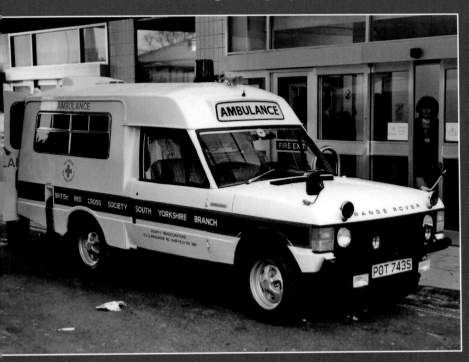

This is the same Wadham Stringer ambulance as in the picture above, right. It served in South Yorkshire. (Author's collection)

This 1984 Wadham Stringer vehicle served in Wiltshire, and has since been preserved. It was pictured at Land Rover's 65th Anniversary celebrations in 2013. (Jaguar Land Rover)

When demand arose for an even bigger ambulance, Lomas rose to the challenge with this design on the 135-inch wheelbase chassis. Despite the very English setting, this is a left-hand-drive vehicle destined for overseas. (Herbert Lomas)

In the mid-1980s, the Emil Frey coachworks in Switzerland built a number of these elegant ambulances on the 135-inch wheelbase. The company was part of the Emil Frey group that also held the Swiss Land Rover franchise at the time. (Emil Frey Group)

Probably the longest-ever two-axle Range Rover was the 139-inch size created by Heinel in Sweden for its ambulance. The host two-door Range Rover was given an extra metre of wheelbase, two new side doors, and a raised roof. (Author's collection)

The Ibis ambulance design was submitted for Land Rover approval in 1972, but appears not to have been successful. The body was unusual in that it was built on a standard 100-inch wheelbase with a greatly extended rear overhang to get the necessary interior space. (Tony Poole)

The Land Rover Discovery was introduced in 1989 as a third product line for the company, positioned between utility Land Rovers and Range Rovers. Its purpose was to give Land Rover a new strong-selling model to counter the anticipated slow-down in Range Rover sales after 1990, by which time that vehicle would be 20 years old, with a new model still several years away. It was also intended to give the company an entry into the newly-emerged family 4x4 market. The Discovery rapidly became the company's best-seller.

To save development time and costs, the Discovery was based on a Range Rover chassis. It was given a new body with distinctive stepped roofline that gave headroom at the rear for two extra passengers, and could be configured as a five-seat or seven-seat passenger carrier. There were 'lifestyle-oriented' three-doors only for the first year, the stronger-selling five-door model being introduced in 1990; door count included the tail door to help differentiate Discoverys from Range Rovers. The model was face-lifted in 1994 with new front and rear details, and a revised interior that could be had with twin airbags.

Land Rover Special Vehicles developed an extended-wheelbase Discovery that was intended primarily as an ambulance, but this was a slow seller. From 1993 there was also a three-door Discovery Commercial (van) variant, but the model was not otherwise developed to provide a range of commercial options. Nevertheless, a few special commercial conversions were made outside the UK.

The primary Discovery power unit was always an economical turbocharged and intercooled direct-injection 2.5-litre diesel with 111bhp. This came as the 200Tdi until 1994, and thereafter as the more refined 300Tdi . The main petrol option was the V8, a 144bhp 3.5-litre with carburettors for the first year, a 163bhp injected 3.5-litre until mid-1993, and then a 180bhp injected 3.9-litre. From 1993-1997, there was also a relatively rare 134bhp 2.0-litre petrol four-cylinder 'Mpi' model, with an adapted Rover car engine. Five-speed manual gearboxes were the norm, but four-speed automatics became available for V8s from 1992, and for diesels a year later.

The first-generation Discovery (latterly called a Series I) was replaced in mid-1998 by the Discovery Series II.

FIRE APPLIANCES

By the time of the Discovery, Land Rover Special vehicles was concentrating its fire service efforts on versions of the utility models, soon to become Defenders. So there was no clear promotion of the Discovery for fire service use. Nevertheless, some examples of the model were taken on by fire services as command and control vehicles.

This early three-door Discovery was taken on by the Northumberland County Council Fire and Rescue Service as an incident command and control vehicle. (Roger Conway)

The volunteer fire service (Bombeiros) at the tourist resort of Faro in Portugal bought a number of 'face-lift' Discoverys. This one was used for incident command duties, as the inscription 'Comando' on the door makes clear. (Roger Crathorne)

This is another of the Faro incident command Discoverys. The vehicle seems to be almost completely standard – apart from the non-factory red paint and the decals, only a towbar, roof-mounted light bar and front protection bar appear to have been added. (Des Penny)

POLICE VEHICLES

Some British police forces bought the Discovery as a cheaper alternative to the Range Rover, using it for motorway patrol duties. Although the diesel-engined models were not as fast as Range Rovers, they were fast enough for most rapid-response calls. Small numbers of Discoverys were bought for special duties, too. Land Rover also promoted the Discovery to police forces outside the UK, where a number of orders were secured.

The Thames Valley Police took a quantity of Discoverys, of which K729 VWL dates from 1992-1993. Although five-door Discoverys were available by this stage, the force clearly decided to buy three-door models. Note the front-mounted towbar, presumably to aid in manoeuvring a trailer of some kind. (PVEC/Eric McIntosh)

The first Discovery to enter police service appears to have been H748 FDE, which was delivered to the Dyfed Powys Police in 1990. The force was proud enough to turn out its helicopter as well for this publicity photo shoot, and the picture shows an anticipated use of the vehicle by dog handlers. Note that the light bar appears to be on an elevating mast as well. (Land Rover)

The Discovery Commercial was not common in police use, and this diesel example was pictured in the ownership of Gwent Police. The heavy bolt visible on the metal grille inside the rear suggests it may have been used for prisoner transport. The registration number indicates that the vehicle may have started life as a Land Rover demonstrator. (PVEC/Paul Billett)

Police forces were often proud of their vehicles, and Devon & Cornwall Police seems to have been keen to highlight the fact that it owned this example. (Devon & Cornwall Police)

The five-door Discovery became more popular than the three-door with police users, as well as with ordinary customers. This late 200Tdi model belonged to the Essex Police. (PVEC/John Oliver)

Discoverys were operated by the Tyne Tunnel Police. This L-registered five-door model has no rear seats, and the whole area behind the front seats is occupied by hoses and pumping equipment. (PVEC/Bob Chambers)

The Battenburg livery was fairly uncommon on Discoverys, and makes this South Wales Police example look particularly colourful. The wheels are the standard 'civilian' Discovery alloys, and the registration number, M442 FAC, suggests this might once have been a Land Rover demonstrator. (PVEC/Matt Holmes)

The various Italian police forces showed a keen interest in the Discovery, and this example belonged to the Polizia di Stato (State Police). The fairlead of a winch is visible just below the number-plate. (Norman Hinchcliffe)

Land Rover tried to get police forces in France interested in the Discovery, and to that end prepared this demonstrator. It was pictured in the port of Boulogne. (Author's collection)

Thames Valley Police continued to prefer three-door models after the 1994 face-lift. This 1995 model shows the new front end details and, like the earlier Thames Valley Discovery pictured, has a front-mounted tow hitch. (PVEC/Eric McIntosh)

Land Rover was determined to break into the Russian market in the early 1990s, and to that end presented this five-door V8i Discovery (along with a Defender) to the chief of Moscow's Traffic Police when he visited the UK in 1992. It appears to have been the only one of its kind, and there is an unconfirmed story that it was the subject of a car-jacking attempt while it was being delivered in Russia! (Land Rover)

Top left: The striped livery adopted by Lothian & Borders Police is very different indeed from the 'jam sandwich' style favoured in the Midlands and the south. This is a 1995 five-door model. (PVEC/Eric McIntosh)

Bottom left: Yet another approach to police livery is displayed on this Humberside Discovery. The striping was of course fluorescent. (PVEC/Eric McIntosh)

Top right: The all-red rear of the Humberside vehicle has darker red chevrons that do not stand out very much in the daylight but are clearly visible at night. The face-lift Discoverys had additional lights in the rear bumper, visible here on either side of the reflective strip. (PVEC/Eric McIntosh)

Bottom right: The Ministry of Defence Police gave its vehicles an almost conventional 'jam sandwich' livery. This 1995 five-door model was pictured at RNAS Yeovilton. (PVEC/Eric McIntosh)

The Strathclyde Police favoured a traditional approach to livery, too, but this Discovery is interesting for its roof-mounted Nightscan equipment. This was a floodlight system mounted on a folding mast. (PVEC/Jim Burns)

This rear view of the Strathclyde vehicle shows the Nightscan equipment quite clearly. Strathclyde was clearly concerned that the vehicle might be prone to rear impacts when stationary and with the Nightscan gear erected, and so the back of this Discovery has reflective chevron decals and a complement of six red warning lights as well. (PVEC/Jim Burns)

Two different approaches to rear impact protection are seen here. On the right is Strathclyde's Nightscan-equipped Discovery, here with another hi-vis scheme. On the left is one of the force's other Discoverys, with a more conventional rear-end chevron scheme. This second vehicle also has Battenburg side decals and, interestingly, a second light bar on the roof. (PVEC/Steve Pearson)

The Discovery could have a most imposing appearance in the right livery, as this Grampian Police example shows. This is a very late example, registered in 1999 after the first-generation Discovery had given way to the Series II on the production lines. (PVEC/Eric McIntosh)

AMBULANCE CONVERSIONS

The main thrust of Land Rover's efforts to sell its products as ambulances was now behind variants of the utility models. Nevertheless, the company could see a potential market for the Discovery as a paramedic response vehicle, and SVO (later LRSV) developed its own ready-prepared Paramedic Discovery. Probably all of these were built from pre-face-lift models.

Quite early in the Discovery's life, Land Rover also developed a special long-wheelbase Discovery ambulance. This had an extra 16 inches in the wheelbase (so making the dimension 116 inches), and could be converted from either a three-door or a five-door base model. However, the conversion was never popular, even though it was also made available for other purposes.

This early three-door Discovery was used as a paramedic response unit in the Scottish Borders region. (Roger Conway)

This is the Paramedic Discovery in its usual five-door form, and in this case serving with the Humberside Ambulance Service. The vehicle has the standard showroom-specification alloy wheels. (Author's collection)

H711 JRW was the five-door prototype of the 116-inch ambulance, and became a demonstrator for Land Rover. This picture clearly shows that an extra panel has been inserted between the doors, and the roof lengthened to suit. (Land Rover)

The five-door prototype was used for a time by the ambulance service at the Rover Group's Longbridge factory. (Stuart Collins)

J140 OAC was the three-door prototype, and some time around 1993 was modified with a GRP raised roof panel that became standard on subsequent new builds. It eventually served with the St John's Ambulance Brigade in Surrey, and was pictured here after withdrawal and before being turned into a camper. (Author)

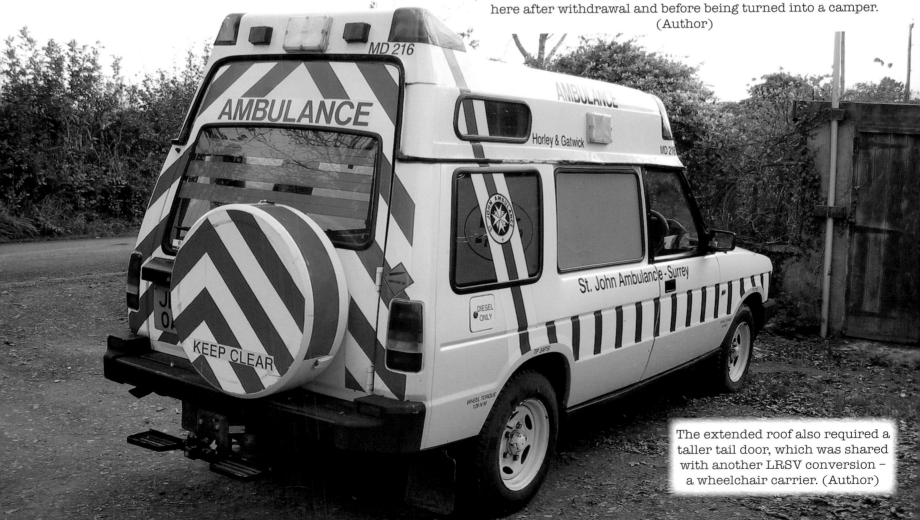

The extended roof also required a taller tail door, which was shared with another LRSV conversion – a wheelchair carrier. (Author)

The front passenger seat was arranged to swivel, so that it could be used by an attendant to supervise a patient in the ambulance body. (Author)

The only major order for the 116-inch Discovery ambulance came from the Northumbria ambulance service, which bought six. All were based on the three-door design. A side locker behind the driver's door replaced the window of the prototype. (Roger Conway)

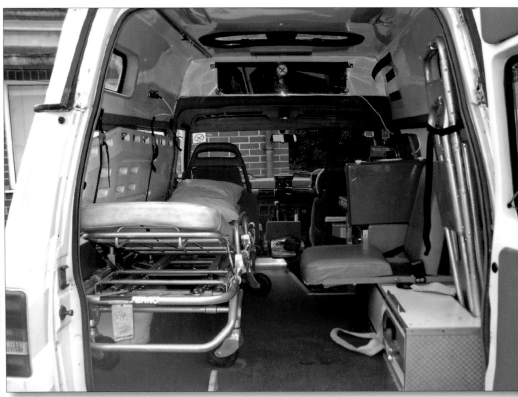

The prototype three-door ambulance was set up to take a single gurney, and had an additional attendant's seat in the rear. (Author)

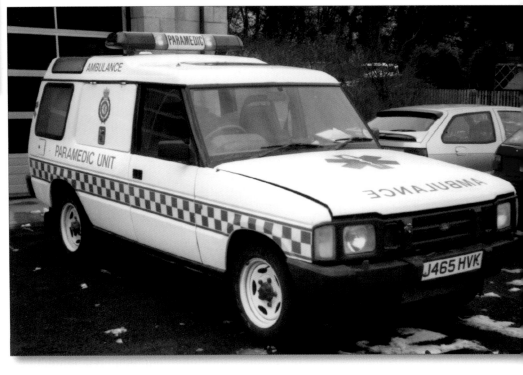

Chapter 8
FREELANDER

The Freelander took Land Rover into a new sector of the market when it was introduced in 1997. Its purpose was to attract former owners of small saloons and estate cars with a Land Rover that drove like those vehicles, but added the marque's attributes of ruggedness and off-road capability. It was always intended as a passenger-carrying vehicle and not as a multi-purpose utility model, although a Freelander Commercial van derivative did become available in 1999. The Freelander was an immediate and massive sales success, quickly overtaking the Discovery as Land Rover's best-seller.

The Freelander was radically different from earlier Land Rovers, with a monocoque bodyshell and all-independent suspension carried on separate front and rear sub-frames. The engine was transversely mounted, and although all four wheels were permanently driven, a torque bias towards the front wheels was achieved by differently-geared front and rear differentials. Instead of a low ratio in the transfer box, the Freelander depended on electronic Hill Descent

Control (which pulsed the brakes through the ABS system to limit downhill speed) and Electronic Traction Control (also operating through the ABS).

When sales began in January 1998, there were both three-door and five-door Freelanders on the same wheelbase. The three-door had an open rear section, and with a folding convertible top was called a Softback, or with detachable hardtop was a Hardback. The five-door was called a Station Wagon. Upholstery was normally cloth, although leather was used on some special editions.

There were two engines in the beginning, a 120PS 1.8-litre petrol and a 97PS 2.0-litre diesel, both with five-speed manual gearboxes. When the Freelander was revised in autumn 2000, the original diesel was replaced by a 112PS BMW 2.0-litre engine (known as a Td4), and an additional 177PS petrol 2.5-litre V6 became available. Automatic gearboxes could be had with the two new engines and were standard with the V6.

The first-generation Freelander was replaced in autumn 2006 by the Freelander 2, which came only as a five-door estate. This had a different drivetrain, still without a low range but this time with a Haldex centre coupling to give automatic selection of drive to the rear axle when conditions demanded. For 2011, a Freelander with front-wheel drive only was also available. Engines were a 160PS 2.2-litre four-cylinder diesel (TD4) or, rarely, a 231PS 3.2-litre Volvo six-cylinder petrol. From autumn 2010 a more powerful 190PS diesel option, called SD4, became available. Then for 2012, a 240PS 2.0-litre petrol engine replaced the six-cylinder, although sales in most countries by this stage were solely of diesel models.

The last Freelander 2 was built in October 2014, and the model was replaced by the Discovery Sport.

The Freelander had insufficient interior space to make a useful ambulance, although some were used as fast-response paramedic vehicles. Land Rover had at least one paramedic demonstrator vehicle, a 2004-model V6 Hardback registered as BF 53 UHY.

FIRE SERVICE VEHICLES

The Freelander, mostly in its later Freelander 2 form, was taken on by several fire services as a commander's vehicle. It was particularly favoured by those services which operated in largely rural areas, where its off-road capability could often be useful. Typically, the base vehicle would be either white or silver, and reflective decals would be applied over this. Modifications would otherwise be limited to the addition of blue lights, fire service radios, and equipment racks.

Not all fire service Freelanders were immediately identifiable as such. This 2011 model belonged to the Hereford & Worcester Fire & Rescue Service, and only the discreet roof-mounted light bar suggested that it was anything other than a standard civilian vehicle. (Author)

The Hereford & Worcester vehicle had its blue lights embedded in the bumper and concealed behind the grille; there was also a blue light concealed within each rear light cluster. (Author)

Hereford & Worcester's Freelander had a dog guard to prevent equipment being thrown forward into the passenger cabin, and all that equipment was stowed in boxes. If the vehicle was responding to a specialist incident, the appropriate boxes would first be loaded aboard. **Inset:** The underfloor space was also used, in this case for equipment likely to be needed at all types of incident. (Author)

POLICE VEHICLES

Land Rover prepared police demonstrator vehicles early in the Freelander's lifetime, and all known examples were diesel-engined five-door types. The company also hoped to be able to interest police forces in the Freelander Commercial, but was largely unsuccessful in doing so.

Freelanders did have an appeal for rural policing duties, where vehicles were likely to spend a proportion of time off-road. They were also sometimes used for specialist roles, such as the Accident Investigation Unit and Crash Investigation Unit roles within a Traffic division. Several were bought by port and airport police services, and there were also sales successes with several continental European forces.

This early five-door Freelander is fairly typical of the vehicles taken on by British forces for rural policing duties. It belonged to South Yorkshire Police. (Roger Conway)

The 2000-model Freelander pictured on the left has the base-specification styled steel wheels that were common on police vehicles. It belonged to the Northern Constabulary in Scotland. (PVEC)

This 2005 model shows the front-end face-lift introduced on 2004 models. Alloy wheels were common on police-specification models by this stage. The vehicle is wearing Battenburg reflective panels, although some of these appear to be peeling off! It belonged to Northamptonshire Police. (PVEC/Alan Matthews)

This 2003 Freelander was pictured on duty at Pendine Sands in South Wales. It belonged to the Dyfed Powys Police. (PVEC/Alan Matthews)

Not every police vehicle was in police livery, and not every police Freelander was a five-door model. This rare Freelander Commercial was used by the Special Constabulary in Colchester. (PVEC/Bob Storrar)

Left: The Freelander proved ideal for port police units. This early five-door belonged to the Port of Bristol Police. (PVEC/Colin Dunford) **Right:** Staffordshire Police operated this Freelander Commercial as a Collision Investigation Unit on the Traffic Division. The Commercial had a plain metal panel behind the door (here carrying the force's crest), where the otherwise visually similar Hardback had a window. (PVEC/Alan Matthews)

Land Rover secured orders from several German police forces in 2003, for both Freelanders and Discovery Series II models. This was a joint publicity picture, showing examples of both types. (Author's collection)

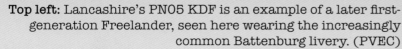

Top left: Lancashire's PN05 KDF is an example of a later first-generation Freelander, seen here wearing the increasingly common Battenburg livery. (PVEC)

Above: The Freelander 2 was again successful as a police vehicle outside the UK. This example belonged to the municipal police at Schaan in Liechtenstein. (Author's collection)

Top right: Rural policing again: this is a 2009 Freelander 2 that belonged to Dorset Police, pictured in Bridport. Light bar styles and liveries varied from one force to the next, in the usual way. (PVEC)

Centre right: Once again dating from 2009, this Freelander 2 was operated by Essex Police. By this time, the Battenburg livery was becoming almost standard among UK forces, although there were still minor variations because force workshops typically prepared the adhesive panels themselves. (PVEC/Alan Matthews)

Bottom right: This 2011-model North Wales Police Freelander 2 shows a variation in base colour. A black vehicle was likely to fetch a better price when sold off after its police service, and with the yellow and blue reflective panels in place was perfectly serviceable for police use. (PVEC/Alan Matthews)

Chapter 9

RANGE ROVER 38A

The second-generation Range Rover was introduced in 1994. Known internally as Project 38A (although the name is often distorted into P38, even by Land Rover), it was larger and much more technically advanced than the model it replaced. Key features were air suspension with height control, and a complex electrical system that served features expected on luxury cars at the time.

There were two V8 petrol engines, a 190bhp 4.0-litre and a 225bhp 4.6-litre, and a six-cylinder BMW turbodiesel alternative with 177bhp. There were initially three levels of equipment specification, and later four, and the trend throughout the model's production life was towards additional luxury and additional cost. Land Rover did not offer any special variants (apart from a police-specification model), and as a result the 38A was never popular with the emergency services. The complexity of its electrical system, which was somewhat trouble-prone in the early days, also deterred aftermarket conversions.

The 38A Range Rover was face-lifted in late 1999, with minor differences to the lights and other details. It remained in production until 2001, when it was replaced by the third-generation or L322 model.

A few 38A Range Rovers were used by fire services as incident commanders' vehicles, but these generally differed little from standard. At the most, they typically had two-way radios, a light bar on the roof, and blue repeater lights in addition to whatever livery the user service applied.

POLICE VEHICLES

The 38A Range Rover was adopted enthusiastically by some British police forces as a direct replacement for their earlier Range Rovers. However, despite Land Rover's provision of a dedicated police specification model, costs were high enough to persuade a number of forces to switch to the less expensive Discovery model. Reliability problems with some early 38As also probably discouraged some potential buyers.

P628 WNL was new to Strathclyde Police. Although it looks much like any other motorway patrol Range Rover, in fact it was bought for special duties, and is armoured back as far as the B-pillar. There were no steel wheels for the 38A, so police-specification models normally had the alloy wheels from whatever was the lowest-specification model of the time. (Jaguar Land Rover)

There was no missing this Warwickshire example with its red decals on the lower half of the body. Different forces continued to take different specifications, and the large blue lights ahead of the grille here contrast with the smaller lights inset into the grille that other forces favoured. (PVEC/Paddy Carpenter)

Greater Manchester Police was an early user of the 38A, and N461 VVW on the right of this picture was actually the first 38A to enter police service. (Nick Dimbleby)

This 1999 model was operated by Cheshire Police. There is a revolving spotlight on the roof, in addition to the usual light bar, and there are blue repeater lamps set into the grille. (PVEC/Eric McIntosh)

The Lothian & Borders Police example pictured here has the 2000 model-year 'face-lift,' with clear indicator lenses and dark 'masks' for the headlamps. The front apron is also painted in the body colour. (PVEC)

AMBULANCE SERVICES

There seems to have been only one special ambulance conversion of the second-generation Range Rover, although some examples may also have been used as incident commanders' vehicles.

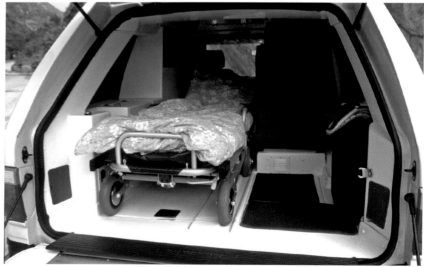

In France, emergency-vehicle specialist Bruno Scherer Entreprise (BSE) turned an early 2.5 DT (base-specification diesel) model into an ambulance. There seem to have been no orders, and the prototype remained unique. (Nick Dimbleby)

The BSE conversion added a GRP 'pod' to the standard vehicle, to give extra length plus a modicum of extra height within the body. (Nick Dimbleby)

Chapter 10
DISCOVERY SERIES II

The Discovery Series II was introduced in 1998, and was very much a refinement of its predecessor. It retained the same overall outline, although in practice no outer panels except for the tail door were carried over. All Series II models had five doors.

A major difference from the first-generation Discovery was a greater overhang at the rear, introduced to allow forward-facing occasional seats on seven-seater models, instead of the earlier inward-facing type. Seven-seat models also had air suspension at the rear, giving automatic self-levelling to prevent the tail dragging if the vehicle was carrying passengers in the rear and was towing at the same time. There was also a sophisticated anti-roll suspension on the more expensive models.

The petrol engine option was a 182bhp 4.0-litre V8 (later increased to 4.6 litres with 217bhp in the USA), but most examples sold in Europe had the 136bhp 2.5-litre five-cylinder

Td5 diesel engine. Both five-speed manual and four-speed automatic gearboxes were available, and there were several different trim levels. Most models had cloth upholstery, although leather was standard at the top of the range.

The Discovery Series II was face-lifted in autumn 2002, with different front and rear details, and some interior changes as well. These later models did not wear 'Series II' badges. The last examples were built in 2004, when the model was replaced by the Discovery 3.

The only special version of the Discovery Series II to come from Land Rover was a Commercial van derivative. Most examples taken on by the emergency services were straightforward conversions of the standard vehicle. A few were taken on by fire services both in the UK and overseas, mainly as incident commanders' vehicles, and some were used by airport fire services, notably by the British Airports Authority at Stansted.

POLICE VEHICLES

Several UK police forces bought Series II Discoverys for patrol duties, and these vehicles often replaced earlier Discoverys. Land Rover provided a basic police specification, but as usual the final equipment fit would be carried out in a force's own workshops.

This 2000-model Discovery was operated by the Northern Constabulary. Like some of its earlier Discoverys, it was fitted with Nightscan floodlighting on the roof. (Roger Conway)

The 'face-lift' specification, with different headlights and front bumper, is seen here on a 2003 model belonging to Kent Police. (Kent Police Museum)

The steel-wheel specification seen here was very uncommon on Series II Discoverys in the UK, where most buyers were interested in the better-equipped models. This is a 2001 model that served with Strathclyde Police. (PVEC)

Land Rover sold Discoverys to a number of German police forces in the early 2000s. This one was operated by the Bavarian State Police. (Christian Bidinger)

Still in the characteristic green and white used by German police forces, but with a very different livery, is this example that was delivered to the Saarland-Saarbrücken Police.
(Jochen von Arnim)

This 'face-lift' example was operated by the Carabinieri in Italy, and was probably used mainly for crowd control duties. Note the mesh grilles on the side windows and the erectable grille for the windscreen, carried on a special bonnet mounting.
(Author's collection)

AMBULANCE SERVICES

The Discovery Series II was sometimes used for fast-response paramedic duties but, like its predecessor, was generally considered too small to make an effective ambulance.

This Series II was operated by the Marins Pompiers de Marseille. This rescue brigade is staffed by French Naval personnel. Despite the red livery that would suggest a fire service vehicle, this one was used for paramedic duties and carries the legend 'Médecin' (Doctor) on its bonnet. (Author's collection/*Land Rover Enthusiast* magazine)

Chapter 11
RANGE ROVER L322

The third-generation Range Rover was developed during BMW's ownership of Land Rover, and was inevitably influenced by the German company's thinking. However, before it entered production in 2001, BMW sold Land Rover to Ford; they also agreed to honour supply of their own parts as necessary for a period of five years.

So the third-generation Range Rover (which took the Ford code of L322) entered production with a choice of BMW engines – a 282bhp 4.4-litre petrol V8 or a 174bhp 3.0-litre six-cylinder turbocharged diesel. Only automatic gearboxes were available. L322 was considerably larger than earlier Range Rovers, with a longer wheelbase to give more interior room. It also broke new ground by having monocoque construction, where both previous Range Rovers had separate body-and-chassis structures.

In step with Land Rover policy of the time, the L322 was developed as a luxury car, and there was never any intention

of making conversions available. Although an emergency-services specification was developed and entered production, the high cost of the new vehicle deterred many potential customers.

From mid-2005, a range of new engines was introduced. A 306bhp Jaguar-designed petrol V8 of 4.4 litres replaced the BMW V8, and a related 390bhp 4.2-litre supercharged V8 was used for a new flagship model. The BMW ('Td6') diesel remained available for another year before being replaced by a Ford-designed 3.6-litre V8 turbodiesel with 268bhp. There were further engine changes in 2009, when the two V8s were enlarged to a 5.0-litre capacity, which gave 375bhp for the standard engine and 510bhp for the supercharged type. By this stage, however, the petrol engines were available only for export.

The last L322 Range Rovers were built in July 2012, when the model was replaced by the fourth-generation L405 type.

POLICE VEHICLES

Despite the additional size and cost of the L322 Range Rover, a number of British police forces chose them as replacements for earlier motorway patrol Range Rovers.

This Cheshire Police Range Rover is a 4.4-litre V8 model with an SE specification. New in 2004, it was withdrawn in 2009 after five years of motorway patrol service, in which time it had covered 188,000 miles. It was then handed over to the force Museum for preservation. (Author)

Below: Force liveries continued to vary in Britain. This is a 2002-model L322 that was used by West Midlands Police. (PVEC/Eric McIntosh)

This 2004 model was operated by Devon & Cornwall Police. The blue repeater lights are set ahead of the grille, rather than within it, as on the Cheshire vehicle of a similar age. (PVEC/Eric McIntosh)

The Northern Constabulary continued to display the force name on the doors when this 2005 Range Rover was in service. There is yet another arrangement of blue repeater lamps at the front, and yet another style of light bar. (PVEC/Dave Conner)

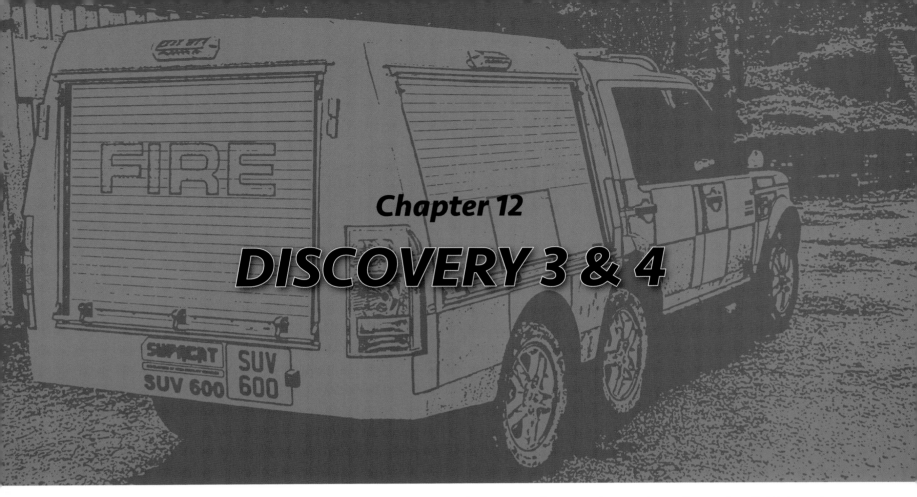

Chapter 12
DISCOVERY 3 & 4

The third iteration of the Discovery range was a larger, more complex and more sophisticated vehicle than those that preceded it. However, it retained separate-chassis construction after the Range Rover (in L322 form) had changed to a monocoque. This was because it shared its chassis and some of its inner body structure with the Range Rover Sport (see Chapter 13).

The Discovery 3 was introduced in summer 2004. Its square-rigged body retained the stepped roof traditional to Discoverys, but now had a horizontally-split tailgate. Most models had three rows of seats, the rear pair arranged to fold flat and provide an unobstructed load area.

All except entry-level models had independent air suspension, with the same electronic cross-linking as on L322. Electronics also underpinned the new Terrain Response system, based on a simple dial which selected the appropriate accelerator response, traction control and other systems according to the type of terrain.

There were three engine options. Central to British and European sales was a 190bhp 2.7-litre turbocharged Jaguar V6 diesel, known as the TDV6. The petrol option was the Jaguar 4.4-litre V8 with 295bhp, and, from spring 2005, some countries outside the UK also had a 215bhp Ford 4.0-litre petrol V6. Gearboxes were six-speed automatics (though a six-speed manual could be had with diesels).

An autumn 2008 facelift saw detail changes and, most obviously, body-colour wheelarch eyebrows instead of the earlier black type. The model was then re-launched in 2010 as the Discovery 4 – essentially a heavily-revised version of the original. A new front end design and detail changes made the vehicle look smaller and less utilitarian, and the dashboard was also redesigned for a more luxurious feel. There were engine changes, too: for most markets, the diesel became a twin-turbo 3.0-litre type with 211PS (TDV6) or 245PS (SDV6). Outside Britain, there was the option of a 375PS Jaguar-derived 5.0-litre petrol V8. Eight-speed automatic gearboxes arrived a year later.

Commercial or van versions of Discovery 3 were available from early 2007, and from the start of Discovery 4 production. These were straightforward conversions of the standard vehicle, with blacked-out rear glass and a dedicated loadspace instead of a rear seat.

Discovery 4 finally went out of production in 2015, giving way to the Discovery 5.

FIRE SERVICE VEHICLES

There were no special fire-service conversions of the Discovery 3 or Discovery 4 available from Land Rover, although some fire services did use examples as incident commanders' vehicles or for special duties. The West Midlands Fire Service, for example, had a Discovery 4 equipped for Technical Rescue work.

Supacat was working on a six-wheel drive system for the SUV600 to make it suitable for airfield duties (where all-wheel drive is a requirement), but there were no takers for the fire appliance version. (Author)

Military vehicle specialists Supacat saw potential in creating a low-profile fire appliance from the Discovery range, and in 2013 revealed its SUV600 model. The prototype was based on a Discovery 3, and the plan was to minimise costs by offering conversions on older vehicles. Land Rover provided support for the conversion to six-wheel configuration. (Author)

POLICE VEHICLES

Land Rover offered a basic police specification for the Discovery 3, and this demonstrator was pictured at a fleet vehicle show. By this stage, it was common practice to use a silver vehicle rather than a white one, because silver vehicles had a better resale value when they were withdrawn from service.
(Jaguar Land Rover)

The Discovery 3 was eagerly accepted by some European police forces, too. This example went to the Belgian Gendarmerie.
(Marc Schrobildgem)

This Discovery 4 police demonstrator was pictured in 2013 while on loan to the Kent Police. (Author)

The Belgian vehicle was a TDV6 SE model, and was equipped with a tow hitch for towing equipment trailers.
(Marc Schrobildgem)

The police livery on the Discovery 4 demonstrator is of course generic, and there is no indication of which force was actually using it at the time. This view shows that Discovery 4 had different rear light units from those on the Discovery 3. (Author)

The capacious loadspace of the Discovery 4 was well suited to police requirements. In this case, the demonstrator vehicle is carrying a few essentials; British forces generally preferred to build their own racking to suit local requirements when they took vehicles into service. (Author)

AMBULANCE SERVICE VEHICLES

Well loaded with equipment, this is a 2008 Discovery 3 in use as a paramedic vehicle by the British Red Cross. Within the Battenburg livery, which was now very widely used, the green reflective decals were used by ambulance services. Fire service vehicles had red sections, and police vehicles used blue. Clear here is the unpainted wheelarch 'eyebrow' of the early Discovery 3. (Jaguar Land Rover)

Not all British emergency-service vehicles carried the Battenburg livery. This 2010 Discovery 4 belonged to the South West Ambulance Service, and was used for fast-response paramedic duties.
(South West Ambulance Service)

As was by now common practice, the South West Ambulance Service created its own racking system for equipment storage.
(South West Ambulance Service)

The Discovery 4's loadspace was well utilised to carry emergency equipment. These two pictures were marked up to assist crews using the vehicle.
(South West Ambulance Service)

There was certainly no wasted space in this ambulance. This is the inside of the left-hand rear side door. (South West Ambulance Service)

In Germany, this Discovery 4 was used by the Land Rover Experience team to provide cover on its Adventure days. (Roger Crathorne)

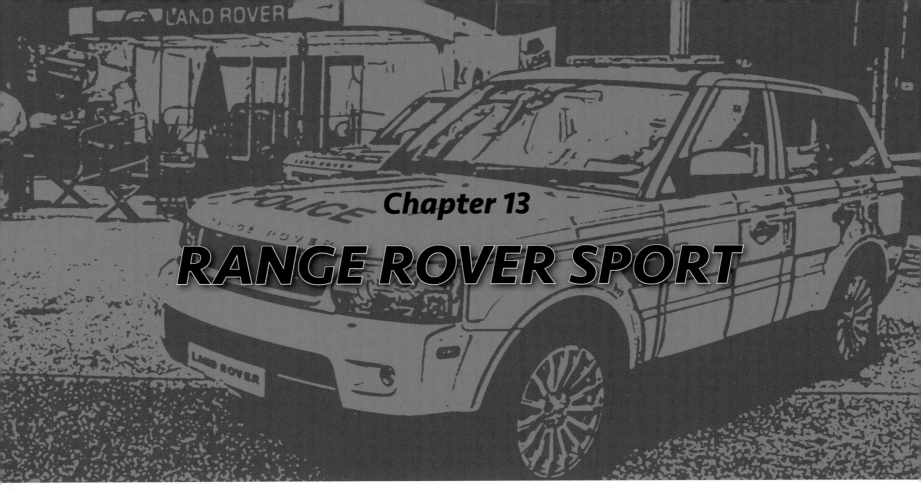

Chapter 13
RANGE ROVER SPORT

The Range Rover Sport was developed for customers who wanted a smaller, sportier Range Rover, with a focus on dynamic performance as well as luxury appointments. Positioned in the product range above Discovery but below the 'full-size' Range Rover, the Range Rover Sport became Land Rover's fifth model line in 2005.

The Sport was based on a short-wheelbase version of the T5 chassis introduced for Discovery 3, and shared some of the same inner body structure. It was offered with a choice of three engines, the headline offering being a 396bhp supercharged 4.2-litre V8; alternatives were a 190bhp 2.7-litre TDV6 diesel and a 306bhp 4.4-litre petrol V8. A 268bhp V8 diesel followed in 2006.

The Sport was always intended as a fashionable vehicle, and

top models tended to appeal to high-profile celebrities. Sales were very strong, especially of the diesel models in Britain. A mid-life face-lift in 2009 was designed to give the model a clearer identity of its own, and to add to its capability, equipment levels, and luxury. It also brought a 3.0-litre TDV6 diesel with 245bhp, and 5.0-litre petrol V8s with 375bhp or 510bhp in supercharged form.

During the period when the Range Rover Sport was in production, Land Rover's focus was on the Discovery as an emergency-services vehicle. As a result, the Sport was never very common with emergency-service users. Although the company did produce demonstrators that carried police livery, this was cosmetic only and was applied to what were otherwise standard showroom-specification vehicles.

FIRE SERVICE VEHICLES

West Midlands Fire Service operated this early Range Rover Sport. It became one of three vehicles used for rapid response to automatic fire alarm calls from hospitals, and the purpose was to reduce the number of false alarm calls that tied up a full-size appliance and crew. An officer in the vehicle would assess the situation and decide whether a full-size appliance was needed. (Jaguar Land Rover)

AG09 YPP was based at West Bromwich and, as this picture demonstrates, carried equipment to deal with small incidents. It was a 3.0-litre TDV6 model. (Jaguar Land Rover)

POLICE VEHICLES

Land Rover prepared this Range Rover Sport as a police demonstrator for a fleet show; it is probably the one that carried the number-plate AK59 HXT. The Sport never did attract many police customers, although there appear to have been some discreetly armoured ones for London's Metropolitan Police.
(Jaguar Land Rover)

MORE LAND ROVER BOOKS AVAILABLE FROM VELOCE:

LAND ROVERS
In British Military Service
Coil sprung models 1970 to 2007

James Taylor and Geoff Fletcher

Land Rover's coil-sprung models include the first-generation Range Rover, One Ten family, Defender family and first-generation Discovery models. All have been taken into service by the British armed forces, and this unique book describes and illustrates their uses and adaptations, as well as containing comprehensive vehicle lists and contract details.

ISBN: 978-1-787112-40-7
Hardback • 25x25cm • 176 pages • 267 colour and b&w pictures

For more information and price details, visit our website at www.veloce.co.uk
• email: info@veloce.co.uk • Tel: +44(0)1305 260068

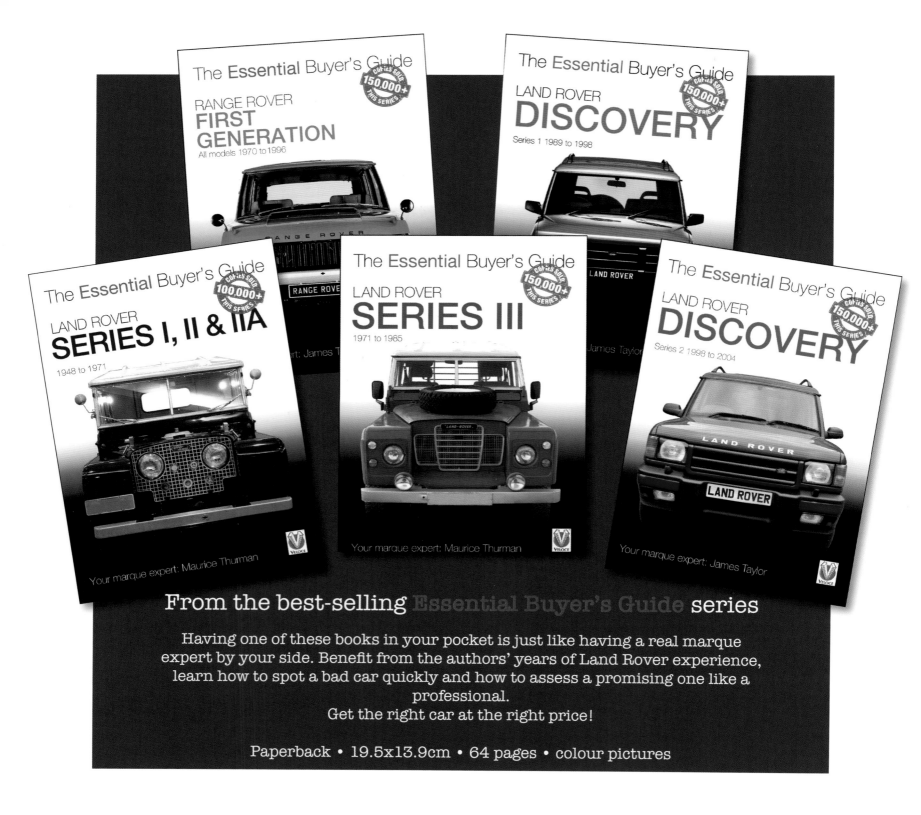

From the best-selling Essential Buyer's Guide series

Having one of these books in your pocket is just like having a real marque expert by your side. Benefit from the authors' years of Land Rover experience, learn how to spot a bad car quickly and how to assess a promising one like a professional.
Get the right car at the right price!

Paperback • 19.5x13.9cm • 64 pages • colour pictures

For more information and price details, visit our website at **www.veloce.co.uk**

LAND ROVER
Series III
REBORN

Covers Land Rover Series III (4-cylinder petrol) 1971-1985
For anyone who wants to restore or improve their Series III, this manual is the essential how-to guide!

Lindsay Porter

Developed from several years of articles in *Land Rover Monthly* magazine, this manual is the most detailed package of information available for anyone thinking of restoring, rebuilding or improving a Series III Land Rover.

ISBN: 978-1-845843-47-2
Paperback • 27x20.7cm
256 pages • 1749 pictures

This book describes the options available for the Range Rover, Land Rover Discovery or Defender, from big wheels and suspension lifts, under-body protection and tuning ideas, right up to how to convert the car into a high speed racer or an international expedition vehicle. With clear, jargon-free instructions, advice on green-laning, international expeditions and competition, this is the definitive guide to getting the most from these exciting vehicles.

ISBN: 978-1-845843-15-1
Paperback • 25x20.7cm
128 pages • 312 colour pictures

SpeedPro Series
How to modify
LAND ROVER
DISCOVERY, DEFENDER & RANGE ROVER
for high performance & serious off-road action

Ralph Hosier

Land Rover Discovery 1989 to 1998, Land Rover 90, 110 and Defender 1983 to 2010, Range Rover 1970 to 1995
Also includes information on servicing, repair, racing, expeditions and trekking, plus a buyers' guide

For all enquiries: email: info@veloce.co.uk • Tel: +44(0)1305 260068

A compact but comprehensive troubleshooter and guide to the Series I, II & III Land Rovers. Common problems are identified, from engine noises to suspension issues, providing easy roadside repairs, as well as thorough advice on more expensive repairs. Covering most models, petrol and diesel engines, this is an essential book for Land Rover drivers.

ISBN: 978-1-787111-16-5
Paperback • 14.8x21cm • 112 pages • 127 colour and b&w pictures

Your Expert Guide
to common problems & how to fix them

VELOCE

Land Rover Series I, II, IIA, & III (1948-85)

Petrol & diesel versions

Excludes forward control, V8, and military models

Your marque expert
Maurice Thurman

Land Rover
Series I-III

For more information and price details, visit our website at www.veloce.co.uk
• email: info@veloce.co.uk • Tel: +44(0)1305 260068

INDEX